Y0-BVN-636

DIFFERENCE
IN TIME

DIFFERENCE IN TIME

A Critical Theory of Culture

NANCY WEISS HANRAHAN

PRAEGER

Westport, Connecticut
London

Library of Congress Cataloging-in-Publication Data

Hanrahan, Nancy Weiss, 1954–
    Difference in time : a critical theory of culture / Nancy Weiss Hanrahan.
      p. cm
    Includes bibliographical references and index.
    ISBN 0–275–96975–4 (alk. paper)
    1. Culture. 2. Critical theory. 3. Aesthetics. 4. Differentiation
(Sociology) 5. Frankfurt school of sociology. 6. Music—Philosophy and
aesthetics. I. Title.
    HM621.H35   2000
    306'.01—dc21   00–022884

British Library Cataloguing in Publication Data is available.

Library of Congress Catalog Card Number: 00–022884
ISBN: 0–275–96975–4

First published in 2000

Praeger Publishers, 88 Post Road West, Westport, CT 06881
An imprint of Greenwood Publishing Group, Inc.
www.praeger.com

Printed in the United States of America

The paper used in this book complies with the
Permanent Paper Standard issued by the National
Information Standards Organization (Z39.48–1984).

10 9 8 7 6 5 4 3 2 1

Copyright Acknowledgment

The author and publisher gratefully acknowledge permission for the use of the
following material:

From *Essays on Self-Reference* by Niklas Luhmann. © 1990 Columbia University
Press. Reprinted by permission of the publisher.

"Without past and future, the present is partial. All time is eternally present and so all time is ours. There is no sense in forgetting and every sense in dreaming. Thus the present is made rich. Thus the present is made whole."

—Jeanette Winterson
The Passion

"... complexity means the necessity of choosing; contingency, the necessity of accepting risks."

—Niklas Luhmann
"Meaning as Sociology's Basic Concept"
Essays on Self-Reference

CONTENTS

PREFACE

The central problem this book addresses is that of critique, an issue with profound intellectual as well as social ramifications. The process of making distinctions and judgments, critique is caught between postmodernism and cultural relativism on the one hand and anti-intellectualism in public life on the other. Questions of aesthetic judgment, as well as of educational standards and standards of public discussion, have become paralyzed in a fruitless debate between universalism and relativism in the academy, and between elitism and egalitarianism in public discourse.

Postmodern theory has had a particularly destabilizing effect on aesthetic and cultural critique. Unlinked from a prevailing set of assumptions about aesthetics (what constitutes the good, the beautiful and the sublime) and suspicious of the liberatory politics that guided marxist cultural theory, the project of aesthetic critique seems to have lost its legitimacy. Indeed, if notions of liberation, like aesthetic criteria, are bound to culture and tradition, why engage in critique at all? What is the basis of aesthetic judgment in the absence of universally applicable aesthetic standards? Can there be an egalitarian or democratic theory that nonetheless makes aesthetic judgments and distinctions? Finally, what is the status of a sociological critique of art, once aesthetic hierarchies are broken down and cultural production is no longer understood to be merely a function of large structures of social control or a reflection of one group's domination? In the face of questions such as these, the argument has been made for a hermeneutic or interpretive sociology rather than a critical sociology and sociological aesthetics. Although interpretation is useful for any critical project in sociology, I believe that abandoning critique would constitute a wrong turn, one based on faulty assumptions about both social conditions and the nature of critique itself.

The argument against critique, within the academy and without, is that it is inconsistent with both democratic political ideals and egalitarian notions of culture. It has been called elitist, unpatriotic or simply indefensible, particularly when it comes to art and culture. Public debate over the National Endowment for the Arts (NEA) is laden with such rhetoric, but the phenomenon is not limited to the cultural field. Universities have responded to the charge of elitism by operating more as credentialling agencies than as institutions that teach students to think critically, resulting in a workforce largely unable to cope with the demands of many new jobs. The idea that what *is* simply is, that there is no point of view beyond the given, has also contributed to a broad disengagement from politics and public life. The attack on critique and on institutions that further it is an attack on all forms of endeavor (including scientific research, aesthetic innovation and political activism) that proceed by generating different and potentially more complex understandings of the world, which are then subject to further critique and revision. In response, the aim of this book is to revitalize critique, to address the charge of elitism by making critique responsive to questions of difference and, in so doing, to reaffirm its place in democratic life. For many of us, culture presents the first public opportunity to exercise critical skills, to make choices, evaluate and decide, and it remains the most accessible realm in which to hone those skills.

I began work on this book, in the broad sense, when I was program director for New Jazz at the Public, a concert series of jazz and experimental music at Joseph Papp's Public Theater in New York. The problematic position of critique in public discourse about the arts and culture readily became apparent to me as I produced concerts, followed the reviews and, all too frequently, argued with the critics. My first research was done in that milieu and I owe a great deal to the many musicians whose work I presented and to the writers and critics, among them Bob Blumenthal, Howard Mandel and Jon Pareles, who provided me with insight into the workings of their profession and hours of engaged debate on the status of critique.

More recently, I have been fortunate to have had at my side numerous colleagues, teachers and friends who have contributed to this project and supported me as I pursued it. Among them, I am particularly indebted to Mark Jacobs and Lois Horton. Mark had the imagination to see the contours of this book long before they had clearly emerged, and its final presentation owes a great deal to his critical vision and insight. If I am really, really lucky, I will have the benefit of his wisdom for a long time to come. Lois made sure that I never forgot the reasons that I wanted to write this book, and that the passion that animated it and the commitments that gave it life were present in my thinking and writing. She has been my steady guide through this process, my right hand, my colleague, my friend.

Many other people have taught and inspired me, including Jeffrey C. Goldfarb, who helped me to articulate the critical issues of this project from its very early stages; Andrew Arato, who taught me what I know about the Frankfurt School; and David Burrows, who got me thinking about time. I am deeply indebted to my guardian angels, Vera Zolberg and Magali Sarfatti Larson; and to my colleagues Anne Bowler, Tia DeNora, and Ann Palkovich, whose contributions and encouragement have been invaluable.

I have also been both supported and inspired by my wonderful family. In his own life and work, my husband Kip has the courage to imagine what doesn't already exist, and the will to realize it in his art. He was a constant source of inspiration to me as I pursued this project and has been an unflinching partner in the life choices and risks it entails. The same spirit already animates our brilliant daughter, Leijia, whose compassion sustained me throughout this project and whose strong moral convictions make me proud.

Finally, I owe a tremendous debt of thanks to my parents, Bertram and Peggy Weiss, whose commitment to my future and whose emotional and material support for this project has been unconditional. Without them, I would never have had the means or the peace of mind to work, and I credit them with understanding how completely the two are interwoven. To my mother I also owe a special thanks for her labor and love in caring for Leijia so that I could devote more time to my studies and to this project. It is with inexpressible love and gratitude that I dedicate this book to them.

INTRODUCTION/FORM

Postmodern scholarship has challenged the premises of grand theory and brought a number of specific concerns to light. Among these, the specific claim that classical theory is based on a universal conception of the human subject that cannot accommodate cultural specificity, or difference, has generated sustained scholarly attention and debate. Certainly, the critique of the classical models in sociology is not new—efforts to incorporate more complex notions of agency and of culture, for example, have been an ongoing feature of the last several decades. But the postmodern criticism goes further with respect to the form of theory itself. Incorporating difference into social theory is not merely a matter of adding something in order to correct an omission. It has involved a more thorough criticism of the way in which analytical categories are organized, social processes conceptualized and theoretical moves structured. It has also challenged the premises of critique in suggesting the possibility of more than one viable standpoint and in criticizing the contingent nature of the aesthetic or ethical categories on which critique has traditionally been based.

Can systematic theory accommodate difference or account for the particular? Will structures inevitably subsume difference? Is

a hermeneutic approach a viable or desirable alternative to a
more critical sociology? Is systematic theory necessary for critique, and if so, how can it be made compatible with more local
or fluid conditions of knowledge? Clearly, the alternatives of systematic theory based on a universal human subject, or hermeneutics based on the stories of particular individuals or groups,
are not alternatives we can live with, as neither one fully accounts for the reality of experience and analysis. Among social
theorists, the call to reconcile the dualisms implicit in these alternatives has been repeatedly made. Yet dialectics, which has
long served social theory as a means of reconciling dualisms and
structuring critique, can no longer fulfill this function. Unlinked
from a defining teleology or any meaningful conception of synthesis, its terms have become reified and its dynamic conception
lost. Dialectical models are not responsive to multiple variables—
recent work that negotiates intersecting differences like class,
race and gender powerfully illustrates the need for alternatives.
As I will demonstrate, the dialectical model of autonomy as a
form of social differentiation has been superseded by the notion
that social subsystems are multiply differentiated not from an
overarching notion of society but from one another. Dialectics as
a basic form of social theory is no longer adequate. Yet the theoretical questions posed by postmodernism are, at bottom, questions of form, including both the nature of structure and the form
of difference. The fact that consideration of form has been missing from the debate between universalism and relativism, structure and difference, hermeneutics and critique, has precluded
any genuine theoretical resolution.

The question of difference and the inadequacy of the classical
models in sociology has posed a particular problem for critical
theory. If critical theory is best defined as "the self-clarification
(critical philosophy) of the struggles and wishes of the age"
(Marx, 1975a: 209) and those struggles have to do with the recognition of difference, to what extent can critical theory still
claim to be critical if it does not, or cannot, take difference into
account? Feminist theorists (Fraser, 1987; Scott, 1989) have suc-

cessfully demonstrated that it is not possible merely to add gender, or women's experience, to existing models; rather, the analysis of gender radically shifts the terms and the structure of those models themselves (Nancy Fraser's critique of Jürgen Habermas being critical theory's case in point). Given this situation, it was necessary for feminists to bring other intellectual resources, including poststructuralism, discourse theory and Michel Foucault's conception of power, to bear on the problem of incorporating difference into systematic theory. In the process, questions have been raised, sometimes explicitly (Fraser and Nicholson, 1994), regarding the degree to which postmodern theory is compatible with a commitment to critique. Yet the issue has not been met with a theoretical solution that examines the structure of critique but through a reiteration of claims to social justice; albeit, in the case of feminist theory, on the somewhat different terms of gender equality.

It is difficult to make those claims with respect to art and culture. Until now, the aesthetic project of critical theory has not undergone the kind of reevaluation described above—largely, I believe, because questions of aesthetic judgment no longer have recourse to an emancipatory or ethical discourse on which to base validity claims. Nevertheless, it is aesthetics that most directly entertains questions of form and can therefore speak to the broadest theoretical concerns. In other words, rather than being abandoned as without justification, the aesthetic project remains the best possible means of elucidating and reinventing the structure of critical social theory. In this book, I argue that the commitment to critique can be compatible with the commitment to difference, and I undertake the detailed theoretical reconstruction necessary to realize that possibility with respect to art and culture. This is accomplished by means of a new temporalized form, modeled on music, which works against the reification of both aesthetic categories and the dialectic itself. Critique and difference are compatible not only on the plane of social justice but also in that their forms are temporalized.

CULTURAL CRITIQUE

For the Frankfurt School critical theorists, art and culture were important components of the critique of modern forms of domination. Fascism made powerful use of aesthetic media for purposes of mass mobilization, but art also had the potential to be a form of critique. To the extent that aesthetic processes could be differentiated from social steering mechanisms, or aesthetic forms differentiated from the logic of domination, art kept open the possibility of autonomous or critical reason itself. In conditions of total domination, then, art was an important link to eventual collective freedom or the constitution of a just society. Hannah Arendt also wrote eloquently on the relationship between art and democratic politics. For Arendt ([1954] 1977a), art and politics share the public realm and, drawing on Kant, are linked through the faculty of judgment. Jeffrey C. Goldfarb picks up this line of reasoning in his analysis of student theater movements in Poland (1982) and the cultural politics of the United States (1991). In east central Europe, critical reason was sustained, despite state censorship, in aesthetic forms such as the student theater that became the basis of the Velvet Revolution of 1989. Even in less repressive circumstances such as in the United States, Goldfarb argues, democracy and critique, including the critique of art and culture, are mutually reinforcing projects. The capacity for judgment, for which art presents frequent opportunities, is a critical skill necessary for democratic participation.

It has long been part of American political culture that an informed and educated citizenry, capable of making judgments, is essential to the functioning of democracy. Yet contrary to the arguments outlined above, judgment about art and culture has more often than not been seen as fundamentally undemocratic. In public discourse, as well as in a great deal of contemporary scholarship, there is a tension, if not a hostility, between cultural critique and democratic practice. This phenomenon reaches as far back as Alexis de Tocqueville's observations of American democracy in the 1830s, but we needn't look further than the recent debates about the NEA to frame the issues. On the one hand, there is the historical construction of the arts themselves as an elite project, which is compounded by the exclusion of the public from decisions about public art and public spending for art. Although the public is excluded from decisions about most other types of federal spending, what is acceptable with respect to foreign policy or matters of national defense is unacceptable in matters of taste. On the other hand, within the arts community, the process and the criteria for judgment about arts funding frequently has been contested. The closed NEA selection panels have been accused of cronyism, of constituting and reproducing an elite of those already funded and already successful. What is different, in the sense of new and untried or sufficiently unconventional to defy the rigid structure of funding categories, often falls through the cracks. NEA controversies concerning issues of public morals have been only the most visible in a long and contested history, and there are many different issues at stake.[1] However, most raise questions about aesthetic judgment or cultural standards as elite practice that is antithetical to democratic notions of participation and inclusion.

The question of the autonomy status of art and culture functions behind most of these arguments as well as of academic debates about art and cultural critique. Is art or culture a realm apart? Do we need to be experts or to rely upon experts in order to appreciate art or to make judgments about it? Are aesthetic forms embedded in larger social processes, or do they follow their own internal logic? Do aesthetic categories reproduce social hierarchies or dominant ideologies? For the Frankfurt School, Arendt and Goldfarb, the potential of art as critique or as a meaningful component of democratic politics is rooted in its potential to be autonomous, in the fact that it is distinct from other types of formal reason and structures of social control. As such, it provides a vantage point from which the critique of social processes can be conducted. Yet it is the autonomy status of art that is called into question whenever expert judgment conflicts with popular morality or notions of taste.

The argument for aesthetic or cultural autonomy as a basis for critique has also proven difficult to sustain given contemporary forms of aesthetic production. In academic circles, the Frankfurt School critique of mass culture has been central to this debate.[2] Part of the Frankfurt School's project of cultural critique was that of unmasking the hidden interests embedded in the production of cultural forms. Mass culture appears in this critique as the reproduction of the ideology of capitalism or as the production of cultural commodities indistinguishable from commodities of any other type (see "The Culture Industry: Enlightenment as Mass Deception" in Horkheimer and Adorno, [1944] 1972). As such, it has no autonomy from social steering mechanisms and therefore cannot provide a basis for critical reflection. Contemporary scholars have criticized this premise on the grounds that culture that is mass produced, that is embedded in social production processes, is nevertheless subject to multiple readings (Radway, 1984). Reception is a free activity that can subvert the manipulation of the culture industry (Fiske, 1987; Frith, 1996). Liberatory or critical possibilities are therefore always available in culture, as meanings are contested rather than simply received. In sum, critical activity is not linked to the autonomy of culture itself.

In addition, the terms of aesthetic autonomy have become associated with reified notions of "high art" and cultural elitism. This is clearly a reductive interpretation of either Herbert Marcuse's or Theodor Adorno's work. However, there is some basis for confusion, in Adorno's writings in particular, given the analytical problems of a dialectical and highly unstable notion of autonomy (discussed in Chapter 1). However viable on its own terms, this argument against autonomy intersects with another strand of debate: the critique of "universal" categories of aesthetic excellence in the name of difference. According to this argument, autonomous art, like high art, is not a universal or transcendent category but one which is both historically contingent and socially produced. If autonomy is not universal, if it can only be determined with respect to specific production circumstances and specific aesthetic forms, how can it serve as a basis for critique? Similarly, if aesthetic standards are variable and contingent, or culturally relative, then on what grounds can critique be conducted?

Outside of the halls of public administration, the specific issue of diversity is at the center of public debate about cultural standards and cultural production. Whose standards are these, and how have they gained legitimacy? Whose tradition or viewpoint is incorporated into the canon of Western literature? What guides curatorial decisions—equal representation of social groups, or transcendent standards of aesthetic judgment? Can a white film director legitimately make a film about blacks? Whereas filmmakers like Spike Lee and scholars like bell hooks (1999) have argued for forms of cultural relativism, conservative critics Allan Bloom (1987) and E. D. Hirsch (1987) link the decline of American culture to a lost faith in universal standards. Again, art and culture participate in a broader debate about the nature of a democratic society. Universalism and relativism are competing frameworks for conceptualizing not only cultural objects and categories but also the structure of pluralism. Yet these discussions have had a particularly destabilizing effect on cultural critique insofar as they underscore the contingency of critical categories. A competing argument for the compatibility of contingency and critique is first presented in Chapter 2 and becomes a central theme of the text that follows.

The concept of aesthetic autonomy was targeted as a central problem of cultural analysis by Raymond Williams (1958, 1961), setting the stage for later scholars in cultural studies. Culture is not the best that has been produced or the court of highest appeal; it is something people make, live in and contest (Fiske, 1992; Willis, 1977). The debate about autonomy has also informed the production-of-culture approach in sociology, including the work of Pierre Bourdieu (1993, 1984), Richard Peterson (1978) and Diana Crane (1992), all of whom suggest that in the last instance, it is the socioeconomic factors of aesthetic production that are determinant. Hal Foster (1983) and Terry Eagleton (1990) represent the effort in postmodern aesthetics to dismantle the category of the aesthetic as a reification of both social relations and scholarship. In music, Rose Rosengard Subotnik and Susan McClary (Leppert and McClary, 1987) criticize the notion of autonomy as a legitimating ideology of conventional forms of musicological research.

There is no question that the concept of autonomy has proven extremely problematic and that its reconsideration has enabled many useful forms of cultural analysis. Whatever Adorno's intention, it has become a reified category that poorly serves sociological analysis or aesthetic critique. Nevertheless, debunking the autonomy status of art altogether leaves theory without a means of either describing social conditions or engaging in critique. Art is both social and retains its distinction from other aspects of social reality. The question, then, is what is the form of this distinction? Autonomy is not an either/or proposition; even Adorno's dialectical conception avoided the stark alternatives of an aesthetic realm untethered from society and a realm of culture completely embedded in society. Furthermore, without some notion of differentiation, the possibility of alternatives upon which critique depends is lost. It is one of the ironies of postmodern theory to have raised the question of difference but at the same time eliminated it in the dedifferentiation of social domains. Autonomy is a highly contingent distinction, yet one that is continually rearticulated in social discourse and social practice. Every time someone in a museum or gallery whispers to her companion, "But is it art?" the issue is raised again. The theoretical problem this book addresses is how can theory manage contingency—indeed, incorporate it into its very structure— and yet retain forms of distinction appropriate to critical analysis? Temporality is the key to resolving this dilemma.

MUSIC AS MODEL

In what follows, music serves as both the model for theory and its object. Though perhaps the most difficult case for theory based on its dynamic and abstract character, music is a model of temporalized form which suggests new ways of conceptualizing both structure and difference. Its temporality is compatible with the dynamic character of social processes and works against the reification of categories that has been part of the postmodern criticism of theory itself. The contingency of the musical object and the social processes through which it comes into being, the nonlinguistic structure of musical meaning and a notion of musical practice as communicative, function as premises of theory construction. The process of theory construction itself proceeds through a series of translations from music to theory and back again to music.

The question, of course, is which theory? Throughout the text, Theodor Adorno's work provides the impulse to critique, as well as its theoretical and practical commitment. However, while Adorno did theorize about music and did use music as a model for history (Hanrahan, 1989) or theory (Buck-Morss, 1977), his specific analyses of music have not stood up to extensive contemporary criticism. Rather than using Adorno's work as a model for the sociological analysis of music, then, it appears in the text as a singularly important model for aesthetic critique. Yet it is a model that is also flawed. As I demonstrate in Chapter 1, the dialectical form of critique which Adorno used has become reified and cannot accommodate a more dynamic conceptualization of distinction and form. Therefore, in order to realize critique, to address its critics, and to contend with issues of diversity, new concepts have to be brought to bear. The notion of contingency as a form of differentiation, complexity as a description of social systems and temporality as constitutive of sociology's subject matter are newly applied to the question of critique using components of contemporary systems theory.

The theory of open systems has a conceptual affinity with mu-

sic in that it is an eventful or dynamic model of social reality in
which contingency and communication are among the primary
analytical categories. In addition, meaning appears in systems
theory not as a specific content but as a system function, which
has a strong affinity with the nonlinguistic and processual character of musical meaning. I am not suggesting that systems theory can function as a replacement paradigm for critical theory;
rather, that a selective utilization of some of these ideas can serve
in the construction of new theory. Contemporary systems theory,
such as Niklas Luhmann's, is distinguished from classical systems models in that it is based on open rather than closed systems. Neither the Parsonian model of a social system as an
integrated whole, the existence of which is ensured by the order
of the parts, or Habermas's conception of social systems as co-
ordinated through instrumental forms of rationality are utilized
here. In fact, what results from this series of translations to and
from music may no longer, in the final analysis, be a systems
theory, much less a systems theory as conventionally understood.

Despite the seeming incompatibility of Adorno's work with
Luhmann's, or of critique itself with a conception of systems,
some of the utility of systems theory is prefigured in Adorno.
At the risk of drastic oversimplification, in Adorno's sociology
of music, music appears as an actual site of social relations,
rather than as a reflection of social relations going on elsewhere,
or as an analogue to some larger social process. In his philosophy
of music, music is theorized as composition, and musical meaning is specifically articulated as compositional process (Hanrahan, 1989). Both of these ideas, the temporalized conception of
music and meaning, and the notion of music as a set of both
social and compositional relations, have informed my thinking,
although neither appears here in its original form. As a site of
social relations, Adorno's thinking converges with a notion of
system; as compositional process, music is understood as inherently dynamic. In a sense, I use Luhmann's work to rescue

Adorno's from the problem of reification, and to fulfill the promise of his critical theory of culture.

OUTLINE

In Chapter 1, I consider autonomy as the form of differentiation utilized in the Frankfurt School's critical theory of culture. Autonomy provided a basis for critique in that differentiation created a space in which alternatives could arise. Yet its form, the negative dialectic, was paradoxical and eventually became reified. As a result, it no longer serves the same critical function. Next, I consider contingency as a replacement form. Because it is dynamic, contingency as a form of difference is not subject to reification but frames differentiation as an ongoing process. Difference is never settled once and for all but is continually being articulated. In Chapter 3, I take this model of social differentiation and apply it to an analysis of music as a functionally differentiated social system. In the process, the basic categories of sociological aesthetics—the work of art, meaning, and production—are radically transformed and brought into line with more contemporary conceptions of their contingency.

In Chapter 4, I return to the specific question of critique. I respond to Max Horkheimer and Theodor Adorno's dilemma of how to conduct critique from within (a totalizing social system, the categories of Enlightenment thought) through an elucidation of the temporal structure of critique. Using contingency as the form of differentiation and complexity as a description of social systems, I re-create the space for critique within systematic theory. Finally, in Chapter 5, I draw out the implications of my work. First, I apply temporalized categories and a conception of critique as contingent process to the analysis of a number of musical examples. Then I consider some of the broader implications of my work through a discussion of specific problems in cultural analysis and a consideration of the problem of structure and difference in feminist critical theory.

In conclusion, I address the question—What is the appropriate form for a critical theory of culture? Not until this theoretical problem is resolved is it possible to revisit the debate between universalism and relativism, structure and difference, critique and contingency with fresh insight, and to create the space for critique both within theory and in public discourse about the arts and culture.

NOTES

1. For an illuminating look at the way these debates played out over issues other than public morality, see Casey Nelson Blake's (1993) analysis of the controversy over Richard Serra's "Tilted Arc."

2. Certainly there are many other points of reference for this debate, including Jose Ortega y Gasset's *The Revolt of the Masses* (1932), Hannah Arendt's "The Crisis in Culture" ([1954] 1977a) and Daniel Bell's *The Cultural Contradictions of Capitalism* (1976), which link mass culture with the decline of culture per se. However, the Frankfurt School most directly links the problem of mass culture with the problem of critique.

1

AUTONOMY

The critique of art and culture has lost a great deal of its legitimacy over the last few decades, both within the academy and in public discourse. The fact that aesthetic categories and distinctions are historically contingent and socially produced has undermined any notion of transcendent standards of aesthetic value that can provide reasonable grounds for critique. What is more, these same distinctions have served historically to support social hierarchies and cultural elites, which makes them particularly suspect as a basis for sociological analysis. Popular understanding and recent public debate about the arts and culture in the United States both reflect and precondition these concerns. "Culture" was historically the preserve of an elite; to be cultured meant that one had enough leisure time for the cultivation of the mind or the senses, which could occur only if one was freed from the necessity of work. The democratization of culture in the contemporary period—propelled by the spread of literacy, techniques of mechanical reproduction and wider access to cultural institutions—has changed this, opening up the realm of culture to those less propertied as well as reflexively changing the very definition of culture. However, democratization coexists, and frequently conflicts, with notions of elite culture, not only with respect to matters of aesthetic judgment but also as competing institutional domains. In this environment, the critique of art and culture is suspect both as a holdover from elite culture of the past and as a form of expertise. The democratization of culture has meant that expertise in matters of aesthetics is no longer the mark of the cultivated individual; on the contrary, the principles which once provided the grounds for aesthetic judgment have little bearing on more popular notions of taste. By extension, the critique of art and culture has repeatedly been attacked as inconsistent with both democratic political ideals and egalitarian notions of culture.

In essence, aesthetic critique is considered problematic because it is ideological, in that distinctions between artworks or cultural practices are based on socially legitimated cultural hierarchies yet presume a universalist viewpoint; or because it is nonegalitarian, in that it makes distinctions at all. Given this analysis, it has been discredited as insensitive to cultural differences and largely abandoned in favor of a more hermeneutic approach to questions of art and culture. The irony, of course, is that this very argument is itself a critique, though one that denies its own conditions of possibility. It is a critique of universalism in the name of difference; but at the same time that it renounces foundationalism, it uses difference as a foundational concept.[1] Certainly, postmodern scholars continue to criticize existing social institutions (including cultural ones), forms of domination (including those of cultural categories), as well as ideological constructions; indeed, these critiques are at the very heart of their work. However, they have left the status of critique very much in question.

The fact that critique is ongoing, whether or not its epistemological status is clear, suggests that it is not the project of critique itself that is problematic but rather the specific claims that can be made with respect to art and culture. Social or political critique is most often based on universal principles of human freedom and social justice, which are difficult to dispute. On the other hand, aesthetic critique does not have recourse to the same moral or ethical grounds for its validity claims. Indeed, questions of morality have had, at least in the modern period, a very tendentious relationship to the arts. In addition, relativism with respect to culture seems to be far more acceptable than relativism with respect to social justice. But this is a dangerous position. If it is elitist to make judgments about culture, why is it not elitist to make judgments about political systems and forms of domination? And if the latter are legitimated or reproduced through cultural media and aesthetic representation, does not the critique of art and culture become central to the very issues of freedom and social justice that frame other types of critique?

The premise of this chapter is that it is not the project of aesthetic critique per se, but the specific forms in which it has been conducted that have become problematic, given more contemporary conditions of cultural production and cultural democracy. Therefore, rather than abandoning critique as an inherently elitist project, I propose that it be revised or reformulated with new questions in mind. The criticisms that have arisen in contemporary scholarship and public debate must be engaged, not dismissed, in the construction of a new paradigm of aesthetic critique that is both compatible with cultural differences and reflexive about its own contingency. Autonomy is a central concept in this complex of issues, as a basis of critical categories and strategies as well as of assumptions about cultural expertise. It will be considered here as a mode of articulating difference that structured critique for the Frankfurt School, whose critical theory of culture remains an important point of departure for contemporary debates.

Critical categories are structured differences—whether they are moral categories such as right and wrong, sociological ones such as social reproduction and social change, or aesthetic ones such as form and content. Given that, the specific way in which differences are conceived is a key element in any analytical structure. Critique, in particular, depends on difference, or nonidentity, as an alternative to what already exists. Questions of elitism and egalitarianism, or historical contingency versus transcendent universalism, engage questions of form as well as of content. Are the categories hierarchically or laterally arranged? Are they dynamic and changing or static and transcendent? Rethinking the form of critical categories based on difference opens up the possibility of restructuring critique as well as deconstructing the rigid dualisms that have stymied analysis and paralyzed public debate.

AUTONOMY / DISTINCTION AND FORM

The Frankfurt School model of aesthetic critique has remained compelling, given the sophistication with which it entertains both formal aesthetic questions and issues of social context or constraints. Its elaboration was based on two fundamental propositions. In order to conduct cultural critique, art and culture had first to be articulated as objects of sociological analysis, and their social domains differentiated from society as a whole. Second, a foothold for critique had to be established vis-à-vis the object that was consistent with the structure of cultural theory and legitimated by social practice. These two propositions remain central to any critical sociological framework. What is the object of critique? More specifically, how do we articulate aesthetic objects in their social complexity? How do we frame the distinction between aesthetic objects and practices and other aspects of social reality, even as we understand them to be inherently social? Second, how do we construct a standpoint for critique? On what grounds do we base validity claims about art and culture? Is it possible to establish a critical distance from social steering mechanisms, which function both as material constraints on production and as ideological constraints on consciousness or subjectivity itself?

These two sets of questions are intertwined in Theodor Adorno's cultural criticism and sociological critique of music in that the distinction between the aesthetic object and society per se is the basis for critique. According to Adorno, only the cultural or musical object could provide a site for the critique of its social mediations. The object cannot be reduced to, or seen as a mere reflection of, other social processes for if it is lost to analysis in this sense, there is no grounding for its critique. For example, Adorno describes the specific alterations of musical composition that are a result of their transformation into commodities. Fetishization—manifest in the star principle, the best seller, the cult of the voice, or of the master violin (Stradivarius)—also generates new arrangements in which familiar themes are repeated to help with product identification, climaxes are emphasized for heightened stimulation, and performance becomes "the barbarism of perfection" ([1938] 1982: 284). In other words,

The works which are the basis of the fetishization and become cultural goods experience constitutional changes as a result. . . . Not merely do the few things played again and again wear out, like the Sistine Madonna in the bedroom, but reification affects their internal structure. ([1938] 1982: 281)

Without the work available to analysis, these processes of commodification, fetishization and reification cannot be materially demonstrated. As a further consequence, no generic social theory, such as reification theory, can adequately explain music or culture as a social phenomenon. Even a sociology of music has to be a theory of music, rather than a social theory applied to music, lest the critical function of the object be compromised.

The central position or utility of the concept of autonomy becomes understandable in this light. First, autonomy articulates art as a distinct aspect of social reality through the form of the negative dialectic. "Art," Adorno writes in *Aesthetic Theory*, "is the social antithesis of society" ([1970] 1984: 11). Art is not just an opposite, it is identical and non-identical to society; it carries the imprint of society, its empirical "other," within itself. The formal properties of the artwork can neither be reduced to other social indicators nor completely disassociated from them. More specifically, "the unresolved antagonisms of reality reappear in art in the guise of immanent problems of artistic form" ([1970]

1984: 8). Art is autonomous to the extent that it follows its own inner logic, but it represents social relations in its form, which becomes the site of critique.

As a mode of social differentiation, autonomy also establishes a standpoint for critique in that it articulates a distance from social steering mechanisms. The concept of autonomy marks off an aesthetic terrain that is always distinct, and critique arises out of the difference between, or potential difference between, art and social steering mechanisms, art's inner logic and the logic of domination or of commodity capital, or simply art's utopian potential. The potential of art as critique and, reflexively, the critique of art, rests in its autonomy and in the exercise of that autonomy. However, this difference is never stable, never absolute. "Blissfully soaring above the real world, art is still chained by each of its elements to the empirical other, into which it may even sink back altogether at every instant" (Adorno [1970] 1984: 8). There is always the possibility that art will suffer the same fate as mass culture, that its distinction from other social domains will be obliterated. Autonomy, the distinction between art and society, has continually to be reclaimed through the self-conscious exercise of art as critique.

The form of the distinction of autonomy, the negative dialectic, not only articulates the relationship between art and society but also serves as the formal structure of critique. Adorno's method of cultural criticism reproduces the negative dialectic as two positions, one within and one outside the work ([1967] 1981). The immanent position views the musical work within a historical trajectory of aesthetic principles and formal logic; for example, conventional forms of literary or art criticism, or musicological analysis, which view the work solely from within an aesthetic tradition. The transcendent position locates the work with respect to a social, often production, context, and has provided the basis of both the sociological critique of art, as well as, indirectly, more contemporary interdisciplinary approaches to culture. Immanent critique is critique from within an aesthetic tradition or with respect to a specific set of aesthetic standards, which frame a confrontation of the reality of the particular work with a specific set of aesthetic principles as norms. Transcendent critique is critique from a position outside of the formal aspects of the work which unmasks the object criticized through an analysis of the interests encoded in its material production. As a form of ideology critique, it may also have as its target the less tangible aspects of the ideological grounding of the work, such as the reproduction of social relations or structures of thought. It is a confrontation between cultural production as social reproduction, and a transcendent utopia. Cultural criticism cannot be conducted from only one of these positions, but the two are not reconcilable. Critique requires moving back and forth between them. Cultural criticism is strategized as an uneasy tension between transcendent and immanent critique.

The primary distinction of autonomy is also reproduced in a number of secondary distinctions within the critique. Autonomy becomes an aesthetic category per se; autonomous art has different formal characteristics than art that is not autonomous, and has a different relation to social production processes. Formally, autonomous art follows its own internal logic rather than reproducing the logic of domination, that is, the ideology of capitalist social relations. As a result, autonomous art cannot be commodified and is therefore not tainted by the reproduction processes of the culture industry. Further, autonomy also has political content: it is linked to notions of autonomous subjectivity and human liberation. As a primary distinction, autonomy functions as a mode of social differentiation and its form, the negative dialectic, provides the form of critique. As a secondary distinction, autonomy provides the basis for distinguishing between aesthetic objects themselves and for articulating their political contents.

THE CRITIQUE OF AUTONOMY

The critique of autonomy in the contemporary literature has been based, to a very large extent, on problems in the Frankfurt

School analysis of mass culture. Whereas autonomous culture had critical potential, mass culture was considered extremely problematic, if not dangerous, not because it was entertainment but because there was no distinction between it and social production processes. Without that distinction, without, in other words, some measure of autonomy, mass culture held no potential for critical reflection. This analysis has been criticized, first, in that it denies the possibility of a free, rather than an ideologically conditioned, response to mass cultural products. Adorno believed that aesthetic response was in fact built into the products of mass culture, leaving no room for autonomous reflection (Horkheimer and Adorno, [1944] 1972). Second, Adorno's critique is linked to a classical aesthetic, in that only high art could escape mass cultural manipulation (though not all high art does escape), which is difficult to justify as more than an aesthetic preference. Taken together, the critique of mass culture appears elitist in that it denies legitimacy to mass culture and agency to the people who like it. These criticisms have prompted a number of studies of the ways in which audiences subvert the meanings of mass cultural products and symbols, and occasionally use them for emancipatory purposes (for example, Fiske, 1987; Frith, 1996; Radway, 1984; Penley, 1992).

These specific criticisms of the role of autonomy in the Frankfurt School's work have also been linked with a more general argument regarding modernist forms of distinction. As an aesthetic category, autonomy articulates a binary or hierarchical difference between cultural works; autonomous art is not merely different from mass culture but is also the privileged term. There is no such thing as difference, per se; difference always generates form.[2] Yet abandoning autonomy as elitist or hierarchical, regardless of how cogent these arguments may be in the specific case of the Frankfurt School, is not a solution to the underlying analytical problem. Critique depends on difference as a set of alternatives to what already exists, as a tension between distinct possibilities. What is more, we cannot function analytically or pragmatically without already existing distinctions, and we are continually engaged in making new ones (Zerubavel, 1991). If abandoning autonomy means abandoning difference *tout court*, if it suggests that there are no meaningful distinctions between aesthetic possibilities, it neither conforms with social reality, in which these types of distinctions are continually being articulated, nor enables critique.

The alternatives here are not differentiation versus dedifferentiation, or difference versus sameness, but alternatives of form. The original form in which the distinction of autonomy was articulated was the negative dialectic. It is a highly unstable form, in that the distinction between art and society, between aesthetic form and social structure, between autonomous institutions and social steering mechanisms, is always in flux. In Adorno's work, autonomy had to be repeatedly marked out; it was never institutionally or cognitively resolved. Furthermore, it is precisely because autonomy is always contingent that it can be productive of the kind of tension on which critique depends. If the autonomy of thought, subjectivity, or institutions was settled once and for all, if it were safely distanced from the context of society, critique would be irrelevant. Yet autonomy has been both construed by its critics and deployed by theorists, including Adorno himself, as a stable category. Autonomous art is that which is not tainted by mass cultural production, which does not reproduce capitalist social relations or is safely tucked away in the high art establishment. A static notion of aesthetic autonomy has also been reproduced in nondialectical forms of aesthetic critique that appear, or claim, to be conducted from a vantage point outside social relations. These interpretations of the concept of autonomy lend considerable weight to the argument that it is elitist and universalist, but they reflect neither the original dialectical form of the concept nor its intent.

Within the tradition of critical theory, this transposition has to be examined in its own right. Certainly there is a great deal of ambiguity in Adorno's repeated use of both the concept and the form of autonomy, indicating that there is something in the temporal structure of the dialectic that was not sustainable in, or transferable to, actual sociological analysis. There is no question that the totalizing context of Enlightenment reason and social administration in which autonomy presumably functioned was also a factor that constrained the dynamic aspect of its dialectical form. The transposition of the concept by more contemporary scholars may also be attributed to the fact that more attention has been paid to autonomy as a content rather than as a form; that is, the concept has been refracted through the more categorical secondary distinctions (an aesthetic category, per se, or one linked to the politics of consciousness). For perhaps all of these reasons, the form of the distinction of autonomy, the way in which the negative dialectic structured the difference between art and society, has become reified into static aesthetic categories with equally static social referents.

This analysis suggests that critique not only depends on difference but also is dynamic. If temporality is central to the structure of critique, if critique depends upon instability, then a new criticism of autonomy can be articulated. Autonomy no longer serves as the basis of aesthetic critique not because it is elitist but because it no longer structures critique in a dynamic or temporalized form.

A PARADOX OF FORM

Autonomy in the form of the negative dialectic presupposes art and society as subject and object or self and other; that is, as a dialectically related pair. In Adorno's formulation, cultural criticism reproduces this form, as the critic moves back and forth between immanent and transcendent positions. However, autonomy was not only dialectical, it was also paradoxical.

Adorno was well aware of at least one paradox of autonomy as the form of aesthetic critique. While only autonomy ensures critique, it is also responsible for its marginalization. In this context, only art that is autonomous can function as a critique of society, and only the autonomous subject can effectively critique art and other social institutions. Yet genuine aesthetic autonomy

in modern conditions is antinomic, a condition in which the relation between art and critique to society as a whole is severed.
As Adorno explained it, in modern conditions, the pleasurable
or emotive function of art is thoroughly implicated in the mechanisms of the culture industry. Therefore, these materials are
tainted and can no longer be employed in a synthetic manner in
great art ([1938] 1982: 274). The fate of autonomous art in modern society is that it must renounce pleasure to escape the domination of the culture industry, but in so doing it loses its social
base. This was certainly the fate of Schoenberg and his circle,
and there are countless other examples, historical and contemporary, of highly innovative artworks that never find an audience because they are either too difficult to enjoy or to interpret
given the existing frame of aesthetic reference, or they do not
appear to be commodifiable and therefore have no access to the
mass production and distribution mechanisms of the culture industry. In these conditions, art as critique easily becomes resistance in a vacuum.

Oddly, this is exactly the situation that critical theory was designed to address. As a general theoretical proposition, critical
theory situated the subject or theorist within the object domain
of society. This reconstruction of the subject/object model was
opposed to the model of traditional theory, in which the theorist's claim to objectivity was based on a position outside both
society and time. Horkheimer's landmark essay "Traditional and
Critical Theory" (1982) is a critique of both scientific objectivity
and orthodox marxism; the first claimed it could uncover the
universal laws of the natural world, the second the transhistorical laws governing human societies. With respect to the development of theory itself, the implications of Horkheimer's
proposition—that the theorist is situated within object domain
of society—are far-reaching. First, as history changes, or as social
relations change, theoretical concepts and constructs must also
change. Second, changes in the subject imply changes in the object, and vice versa, a notion with broad implications for revolutionary subjectivity. Finally, theory is articulated as a form of

praxis, given that critique would always be situated within social conditions.

Critical theory positioned the subject within the object domain of society yet sought to establish a foothold for critique outside that domain. What resulted was a paradox of form that could never be resolved. Horkheimer and Adorno understood that critique, like any form of knowledge, is always situated, never free-floating. At the same time, it is a specific activity, a process of mediation that requires distance from the object. When that object is society, and the subject is positioned within the object, how is mediation to be accomplished? How is a critical distance to be established? Reflection was claimed to be the mediating activity between subject and object. Yet what, given this formal structure, grounds reflection? This problem receives its most poignant treatment in *Dialectic of Enlightenment*, where Horkheimer and Adorno ([1944] 1972) reflect on the impossibility of critique in contemporary conditions of Enlightenment rationality. If Enlightenment reason is a totalizing form of domination, they argue, then there is no position outside Enlightenment reason from which to conduct critique. In other words, reflection could only occur in the existing categories of Enlightenment thought, which were themselves implicated in the structure of domination in modern society. This paradox of autonomy signaled the end of the project of critical theory in this period. Although Horkheimer had envisioned critical theory as a continuing self-reflection on the changing conditions of its own project (i.e., critique), the publication of *Dialectic of Enlightenment* in 1944 drew that process to a premature, if provisional, close.

In essence, Horkheimer and Adorno postulated two different models of autonomy, both dialectical, that could not be reconciled.[3] The first was an autonomy vis-à-vis society, which pertained to social institutions or forms of rationality such as art. The second was an autonomy within society, which pertained to human subjects and the autonomy of thought. The first was not analytically stable, yet the recourse to a reified notion of autonomy effectively marginalized aesthetic critique. With regard to the second, the autonomy of the subject within society could not be established given the interpretation of the object, society, as a totality. Critique became impossible because there was no subjectivity that was not compromised, and no other foothold for critique in the structure of reality to ground it. In essence, reifying autonomy provided a means of ensuring the grounding for critique, but in the process critique lost its dialectical and dynamic character.

With respect, then, to the question of establishing a standpoint for critique (the second of the two initial propositions for a critical theory of culture), autonomy proved to be an extremely problematic solution. Feminist standpoint theorists (e.g., Harding, 1991; Smith, 1987) and scholars in cultural studies (Bhabha, 1994; Spivak, 1988) have responded by attempting to develop critique from the point of view not of the autonomous subject per se but of a particular subject, situated through identity or ideology. The assumption here is that if the standpoint or position of critique is relativized, critique can be conducted on grounds that both recognize cultural difference and are more egalitarian. Yet it is not at all clear that standpoint positions or subject positions solve the underlying formal problems of critique. Standpoint theories may allow critique to circumvent the charge of elitism by situating it on the correct side of the political line—in the name of the people, or women, or the subaltern. However, in addition to the obvious problems of inverted hierarchies and claiming legitimation only for the oppressed, there is also a serious theoretical problem: there is no standpoint that is fixed. As soon as identities, classes, or locations (positions in space) are formed, they become multiple and mobile; any subject position will generate its own complexity. As every feminist scholar, activist or observer knows, as soon as the category *woman* was formed, it unravelled into middle class or lower class; white, black, Asian or Latina; professional, working or domestic; prolife or prochoice; gay or straight; third world or first world, and so forth. Relativizing a universalist standpoint only reproduces the original fallacy, creating a new category that is as much a fiction as the original. In essence, relativizing the subject or subject position responds to the problems of universalism implicit in the concept of autonomy, but not to the problem of its form. Quite to the contrary, standpoint theory reproduces the reified form of autonomy in assuming that positions, identity or ideology can be fixed. What's missing from this solution is a dynamic model of form that can structure critique as a tension between alternatives; that is, as a temporalized articulation of difference.

THEORY OF THE OBJECT

The Frankfurt School critical theory of culture, with autonomy as its primary distinction and the negative dialectic as its principle form, also ran into difficulties with the other aspect of the project, that is, constructing the aesthetic object as an object of sociological analysis. If one accepts Adorno's premise that the aesthetic object is the site of critique and therefore a theory of the object is essential to any critical theory of culture, the problem of critique cannot adequately be addressed without considering the construction of the object itself. Alternately, Roland Barthes suggested that theory is not applied to the object but concepts are forged from the object, which also gives priority to theory as theory of the object (cited in Bois, 1990: xii). However the argument is framed, the root of some of the problems of aesthetic critique practiced by the Frankfurt School are implicit in the theory of the object as it was constructed through autonomy. The question of static or reified form surfaces here as well.

Adorno's articulation of the musical object through the formal properties of musical composition was consistent with one of the meanings of autonomy, or one of the ways in which art was marked off as an autonomous sphere—that is, art as form of reason or cognition. It is because music follows, or can follow, its own internal logic that it has the capacity to resist, or to function as a critique of, capitalist social relations. The formal aspects of music are of further importance in Adorno's analysis in that aesthetic form is the mediating category between art and society, and therefore the site of aesthetic critique. Yet aesthetic objects are not self-evident as form and cannot be bracketed by purely formal considerations. This is particularly true of music, which is only actualized in a performance, which in the classical music tradition is in turn an interpretation of an already existing composition or score. Nor is Adorno's formalist reading of musical work mediated by his claim that reception is co-constitutive of the work. Prefiguring more contemporary versions of reception theory, Adorno suggested that the work is only fulfilled or realized in reception. However, the listener remains subordinate to the work in that he or she does not freely constitute it through reception but rather only grasps, or fails to grasp, the formal logic of the composition. In other words, Adorno's co-constitutive theory of art presupposed a standard of ideal or expert reception that did not take the contingency of either aesthetic objects themselves or their reception into account ([1962] 1976). This aesthetic argument conformed to a broader tendency within the Frankfurt School to characterize large social and historical processes as teleological, and forms of domination as total, often making their analyses blind to the contingencies of human action and agency as well as to the possibility of anomalous events.

Situating the autonomy of the aesthetic object in the formal aspects of the work resulted in a reification of the concept of autonomy, and of musical works themselves, in the most classic sense. With a single gesture, the formal aspects of music now confront the listener as alien and hostile, and a formerly dynamic notion of autonomy as a dialectical relation reappears as a stable form. The reification of the aesthetic object as a function of classical aesthetics has been the subject of extensive criticism, and while not a direct response to Adorno's work, postmodern literary theory has spoken to this problem. The important contribution that has been made is the recognition of the contingency of art works and reception, both in the sense of their categorization as "works" and with respect to meaning. Rather than a more conventional literary notion of meaning embedded in the text and uncovered by analysis or interpretation, meaning is actively constructed by readers, and texts are subject to multiple "correct" interpretations. This understanding of works and reception is elucidated and situated within a more complete social and analytical framework in Chapter 3.

The autonomy of art as a distinct social sphere was also marked out, and in some sense institutionally secured, with respect to production. Those works that were subject to commodification were implicated in social production processes and served the reproduction of its ideology, experiencing constitutional changes as a result. The transformation of these works into products of mass culture, or the blatant production of culture as a product, was the destruction of their status as art in any true sense of the word. Autonomous works were those that were so formally difficult that they could not be commodified and therefore escaped this fate. Yet the social differentiation of art on the basis of production has also turned out to be rather more complex and problematic than this paradigm suggests. Certainly the culture industry still circumscribes vast areas of cultural production, but a dialectic between it and an ideal of aesthetic autonomy can no longer be constructed. Rather than a model of totalizing whole, which some aesthetic production escapes, the contemporary picture is better articulated as a whole that is comprised of shifting parts. In the broad sense, there is no cultural or aesthetic production that is not subject to some dimension of the culture industry or the market (Bourdieu, 1993). Even the most alternative music requires capitalization to be produced and circulation in a market to be sustained. Nevertheless, to portray the culture industry as totalizing, either as a form of domination or as a production system, ascribes far too much legitimacy to the industry's own claims. Like any highly rationalized process, it is subject to irrationality or unpredictability in any of its moments, producing unexpected results, contingent effects and an astonishingly high rate of failure.

The conception of the culture industry as a totalizing whole that oversees the production of consciousness was criticized early on by members of the Birmingham School. Early work in cultural studies was a direct response to the broad indictment of mass culture and its consumers, in particular the notion that anyone who enjoyed mass culture was ideologically implicated in it. These insights have been supplemented by more contemporary analyses of the industry which demonstrate that it is not a closed system of production but rather one that is open to its environment. To take but two examples, both Todd Gitlin (1985), in his analysis of network television, and Simon Frith (1996), on the music industry, argue that the industry is responsive to audiences or social issues at the same time that it exploits both. Gitlin's thesis is that the networks are in fact highly sensitive to social issues, indeed, their success depends on "their ability to borrow, transform, or deform, the energy of social and psychological conflict" (12). However, these issues or conflicts are represented by network television as the private dilemmas of sitcom stars, which minimizes or altogether obscures their complex social ramifications. Frith suggests that the music industry operates as something of a dialectic. On the one hand, it is audiences and musicians that generate both new musical forms and their popularity, not the five multinational record companies. Like Gitlin, he argues that the industry's success in fact depends on this vitality; the industry "follows tastes rather than forming them" (85). Yet in the routines of mass marketing it exploits taste rather than simply accommodating it. Although they produce very different judgments about the relative openness of the culture industry, both authors suggest a model that is far more porous than earlier analyses had assumed. In addition, contemporary production, even within the industrial model, is highly diversified. The categories of the Frankfurt School analysis could not allow for the contingency of reception, the unintended consequences of cultural production processes or the possibility of a more diversified, and therefore less streamlined, production environment.

DIFFERENTIATION AND TIME

Both the cognitive/aesthetic and the production categories that marked out the distinction of autonomy have proven to be a great deal more fluid than the perspective from the 1940s indicated. Not only, then, is the form of autonomy problematic as the structure of critique, but also the specific distinctions it articulated—the way in which it structured the difference between art and other social domains, and between aesthetics and other formal logics—failed to take the contingency of these categories into account. Given the theoretical and pragmatic tasks that autonomy was supposed to accomplish—providing the only stable basis for critique, as well as structuring the terms of the attack on the culture industry—acknowledging contingency would have been exceedingly risky. Suffice it to say that autonomy articulated its objects in terms that were static. If, on the other hand, contingency is a condition of both aesthetic objects and the social domain of art, an entire range of questions needs to be reconsidered. What is the distinction between art and other social domains? What is the difference that constitutes aesthetic objects, and how can these differences be articulated? Alternately, are these distinctions that still need to be made, or is the situation so fluid that it defies structure?

Certainly it is no longer adequate to conceptualize the boundaries between social domains in reified terms. However, the notion that there are no meaningful boundaries between art and other social domains—or between, for instance, aesthetic objects and advertising—mistakes distinction as a form of difference for distinction as a form of privilege. Boundaries are fluid and contingent, but they have not ceased to exist. As the recent (October 1999) uproar over the Brooklyn Museum's exhibit "Sensation" demonstrates, regardless of the fact that both the aesthetic object and the social category of art are in flux, they continue to structure discourse, practice and social institutions. In these debates, the meaning of art, the purpose or function of social institutions of art and even the grounds on which we should debate art have all been contested. Is art supposed to please or to shock or to make us think? Should it be transcendent or in your face? Where is the line between artistic freedom and social or moral accountability? Do we fund art institutions as a matter of the public trust or on the basis of square feet of exhibition space? Do we talk about religion or the First Amendment, formaldehyde or private fortunes? Art institutions are in constantly shifting relationship to other social institutions, like those of religion and government, and, in the process, the distinctions between them are continually reproduced. In other words, what it is that makes art distinct and whether or not it should be distinct are both fiercely contested. Yet it is precisely that distinction, precisely that specificity, that drives all of the arguments and frames all of the questions.

How, then, should theory articulate the distinction between art and other social domains, given its ongoing contingency? The answer is rather straightforward. If the object itself is in flux, it requires a temporalized language to articulate the form of its distinction. In other words, the theory of the object has to be temporalized. Attention to temporality is also crucial to the articulation of critical categories to the extent that difference is always articulated in time. Difference is never settled once and for all, it occurs and recurs. It is dynamic, not categorical. Difference will never be grasped by reified form, yet it continually articulates form. The tendency in postmodern scholarship to implicate autonomy in the critique of universalism and thereby to dismiss the whole project of critique as unsound is a position taken in the name of difference. However, without attention to matters of both form and time, difference itself cannot be articulated.

Temporality also accords with the structure of critique. Rather than being the rigid application of already existing aesthetic categories, critique is inherently eventful; it is a process of making distinctions. To date, the debate about critique has focused either on standpoint or on the content of critical categories. However, the emphasis on space and content, rather than on time and form, tends to the reification of categories of difference, reproducing the very problem it was meant to address.[4] It also represents an inversion of critique itself in that standpoint does not precede critique but rather is established through the process of critique. It is not the form that produces difference but rather the process of articulating difference, of making distinctions, that generates the form. As an aspect of critique, the form of difference is continually emergent, structuring critique in a very dynamic sense.

Finally, aesthetic critique differs from social critique and cannot be legitimated on the same grounds. However, it does not follow that it is elitist to make distinctions about art any more than it is elitist to make distinctions about politics. What I have argued instead is that aesthetic critique becomes problematic when its terms are legitimated on the basis of fixed positions such as universal aesthetic criteria, an ideologically positioned subject, or a historical teleology; that is, when it fails to recognize or disclose both its contingency and its embeddedness in time. Given the contingency of aesthetic categories and social domains, fluid and dynamic distinctions—rather than binary, oppositional or hierarchical ones—are required. What I propose is to replace the reified form of autonomy with the dynamic one of contingency, as a form of difference for aesthetic critique. Contrary to postmodern logic, contingency is not the death of critique but the possibility of a new form, and the means of making the commitment to difference compatible with the commitment to critique.

NOTES

1. Or, as Craig Calhoun put it, "This emphasis on difference is the most valuable and defensible of postmodernist arguments, though it is not defensible on postmodernist terms" (1995: 115).
2. G. Spencer Brown demonstrates this with a simple exercise (1972: 1). Take a flat plane, such as a piece of paper. Draw a distinction "by arranging a boundary with separate sides so that a point on one side cannot reach the other side without crossing the boundary." It is not possible to draw a distinction without generating a form. Any line

through the plane, whether straight or curved, any shape, regular or irregular, articulates form. Once the distinction is drawn, "the spaces, states or contents on each side of the boundary . . . can be indicated." But there is no indication without distinction and no distinction without form.

3. Susan Buck-Morss's (1977) analysis presents a different explanation of this paradox, suggesting that it arose from the conjunction between Adorno's philosophical and aesthetic notion of autonomy with Horkheimer's more sociological one.

4. Reification of the categories of difference also has important political consequences. See Nancy Fraser (1997: Chapter 1).

2

CONTINGENCY

Social processes are commonly understood to be contingent, in the sense that they are neither overdetermined nor completely random. Although they both occur within and structure given social circumstances, no social process follows necessarily from those circumstances. Similarly, social processes may either conform to or defy historically grounded expectations. As a corollary, the outcomes of social processes are always contingent in that things could turn out otherwise. Expectations can be denied, anomalous or surprising circumstances can arise that affect the outcome and may require a change of plans. Finally, the meaning of social processes, just like the meaning of cultural objects and practices, is contingent upon both history and biography. Meaning is always generated within a context (indeed, it often generates context) and is subject to multiple interpretations.

Contingency, then, is a taken-for-granted aspect of sociology's subject matter, but it often drops out of theory. The search for the underlying laws of human societies, or for the general principles that can be abstracted from particular moments or situations, militates against the contingent or the anomalous. Even Max Weber, whose work is the exception in the classical canon in eschewing general laws of history for the notion of elective affinity and historical accident (Weber, 1930), cannot, in his writing on music, account for the dominant 7, the exception to the rationalization process evident in the system of chordal harmony (Weber, 1958). The narrative structure of theory predisposes us to treat what has occurred as the necessary outcome of particular social and historical circumstances, and although theoretical categories are themselves contingent, changing over time or from one context to another, in their utilization they appear transcendent and immutable. Contingency may be a part of our understanding, but it is not built into the structure of theory or sociological modes of explanation.

If it is difficult to retain contingency within the structure of systematic theory, its relationship to critique is even more problematic. How can contingency be compatible with critique, with moral judgment and principled argument? The structure of contingency appears to be the inverse of the structure of critique— unpredictable outcomes and fluid categories stand opposed to immutable principles and fixed standards. For this reason, contingency is most often linked to relativism. In actual social practice, however, that has not always been the case. As an example, contingency was implicit in the social movements of the 1960s, but they had a strong moral core and were not relativistic. The "situational ethics" that was developed was based on principles but also took the context into account; in different situations, the application of those principles would lead to different outcomes. Debates about a good war, about when violence is justified to pursue moral ends such as racial equality, and about euthanasia are examples of situational ethics, weighing ethical principles against specific situations and their potential outcomes.

Whereas social radicalism was able to blend contingency with a moral core, cultural radicalism has not. The collapse of a universalist notion of aesthetics based on the true, the beautiful and the sublime, and the consistent failure of attempts to articulate political criteria in aesthetic terms, have left aesthetic critique without transcendent moral or ethical grounds. If aesthetic criteria such as beauty and technique are themselves socially contextualized and historically specific, it makes no sense to apply them situationally—they are already situational, relative to a given context. In all but the most specifically political art, as in cases where aesthetic production is subordinate to the needs of the state, the representation of principles such as social equality in aesthetic terms is at best ambiguous and open to interpretation. The difficulty is compounded in music, given its lack of objective content. Not only is there no fully articulated ethics of art, but to the contrary, morality and ethics have had a very contentious history with regard to art. In the modern period, art has often been designed to shock by crossing socially acceptable boundaries. As a partial consequence, contemporary debates about morality and art have turned toward public discussion of obscenity and sacrilege, rather than toward constituting a moral grounds for aesthetic critique.

Recognizing contingency in the cultural domain has led away from judgments and principles rather than to the elaboration of an alternative form of ethics. This is not to say that there is no social criticism of art, but whereas situated aesthetics has come to mean criticizing each work solely within its own frame of reference, debates that do invoke transcendent principles like Christian morality or the First Amendment often have little to do with art itself. Indeed, it is not uncommon for the combatants never to see the work in question. However, if the problem with regard to the arts and culture is to retain principles in the face of contingency, the inverse is true with respect to social criticism. In the most extreme cases, social and political radicalism risked becoming orthodoxy, as contingency was abandoned in favor of rigid principles and their universal application. Relativism in the arts and culture and dogmatism in politics are two sides of the same coin. Certainly the balance between contingency and transcendent principles is difficult to maintain.

By definition, what is contingent is not subject to necessity. Yet contingency is not merely a synonym for unpredictability, nor is it an absolute condition, where what is contingent could be said to be anything at all or where contingent processes are absolutely random. According to Niklas Luhmann:

This concept results from excluding necessity and impossibility. Something is contingent insofar as it is neither necessary nor impossible; it is just what it is (or was or will be), though it could also be otherwise. The concept thus describes something given (something experienced, expected, remembered, fantasized) in the light of its possibly being otherwise; it describes objects within the horizon of possible variations. It presupposes the world as it is given, yet it does not describe the possible in general, but what is otherwise possible from the viewpoint of reality. ([1984] 1995: 106)

Contingency articulates a distinction between what is and what could be or could have been. Moreover, Luhmann goes on to say, any given "what is" is a result of selection from a range of possible variations. Contingency as a form of difference is not one in which differences are determined from a preexisting conceptual or social structure, or pregiven from a specific set of historical, moral or aesthetic circumstances. As they are the result of selection, they could always be otherwise, and there is always an element of risk.

Selection generates "what is" as a distinction from what could be, marking its difference from the horizon of possibilities. Selection is a decision, yes or no, this option and not those, but it is always provisional. Selections do not stop at "what is" but keep on going, continually articulating other circumstances. The distinction that constitutes "what is" is contingent, in that it could have turned out otherwise, but contingency also implies temporality in that the reality of any moment or situation is constantly in flux, as new definitions are generated and new situations arise.

What I am proposing is that contingency be used as a starting point for aesthetic critique. It is a form of distinction that can function as a replacement concept for autonomy and the negative dialectic. The structure of contingency as a difference between what is and what could be (or could have been) corresponds with the distinction between the actual and the potential that is the basis of critique. In addition, contingency is a temporalized form of distinction, which works against the reification of aesthetic and critical categories as well as static conceptions of difference itself. Given that social processes and their outcomes are contingent, incorporating contingency into the structure of theory can enhance sociological analyses of, for instance, cultural production and social differentiation. It also serves in the development of new critical categories appropriate to the contingency of aesthetic objects, meaning and reception.

Contingency is not incompatible with critique, but it does restructure its conventional forms. I will first consider how contingency as a form of difference articulates the social differentiation of art, upon which sociological critiques of culture have been based. Next, I will consider the temporality of form as central not only to the structure but also to the standpoint of critique. Finally, I argue that contingency is linked not to relativism but to judgment, and that aesthetic critique based on contingency carries political responsibility.

SOCIAL DIFFERENTIATION / THE PRIMARY DISTINCTION

To the extent that the category "art" still structures discourse, practices and institutions, the social differentiation of art is an aspect of social reality that will be treated here as given. The theoretical project is to describe and to analyze *how* the category of art functions to organize social practices or communications, or to articulate the distinction between artworks and other social products. What is the identity of the social domain of art? How is art differentiated from other aspects of social reality? Is it institutions that lend this field its integrity, or is it based on objective social relations, a specific set of practices, forms of aesthetic discourse or the sum total of artworks? Is it possible to map out the social domain of art in a way that reflects its shifting boundaries and complex relations with other social domains?

Social differentiation is two-sided. Differentiation is always differentiation from something, or with respect to something, rather than difference in and of itself. What is more, it is through the process of differentiation that the integrity of a social domain is established and that its elements attain their specificity. Historically, the social differentiation of art occurs with respect to other social domains within constantly changing social conditions. These conditions reflexively shift not only the boundaries of the domain of art but also its internal forms of reference.

The differentiation of art as a social domain has never been self-evident in purely aesthetic terms. As soon as art emerged in Europe as a differentiated value sphere, one freed of its religious and courtly functions and able to develop according to its own formal imperatives, it became dependent on the market and implicated in social production relations. Whatever kernel of truth it may have held in an experiential sense, the bourgeois ideal of art as a sphere of contemplation, or of the harmonious reconciliation of subject and object or form and content, was only an ideal, even in the nineteenth century. Not only was the piano in the bourgeois living room or salon a commodity, it was also an indicator of social class. Artworks were bought and sold, their value measured precisely in the ability of their subject matter to transcend the mundane processes of their exchange. Even before the mercantile age, art was linked to status. What was different in the bourgeois period was that it became a mode of attaining social status available to more and more people, and as a result the vocabulary of aesthetic capital changed. In other words, the shifting social context of art was also a constitutive aspect of its content. Religious imagery and courtly depiction gave way to romanticism as a secular form of transcendence, or to naturalism as an exploration of subject matter drawn from everyday life.

In the United States the differentiation of the social domain of art reached fruition in the late nineteenth century with, in Lawrence Levine's (1988) coinage, the sacralization of high art. The development of nonprofit enterprise as a distinct institutional base for high culture accomplished several goals (Di-

Maggio, 1992). Given the democratic tendencies of American culture, it preserved the bourgeois ideal of culture against both incursions from the lower classes and rampant commercialization. Not only did symphony orchestras and noncommercial theater companies perform in different physical spaces than the older music halls, these institutions also prescribed behavior and dress appropriate to the elevated nature of the art form. Much like European museums, which were charged with the dual function of educating or enlightening the populace as well as cultivating their manners, the social domain of high art was not marked out on the basis of aesthetic criteria alone but was reinforced through distinctly social means (Bennett, 1995; Zolberg, 1992). The sacralization of high art and the development of institutions to preserve and defend it were driven by considerations of social class. Yet the ideology of high culture as a sacred preserve obscured the fact that art was still embedded in social and economic processes and that its institutions reproduced broader social tendencies. Adorno's scathing analysis in "On the Fetish Character in Music and the Regression in Listening" ([1938] 1982) is only one possible statement of this argument. According to Adorno, to the extent that high art is implicated in the capitalist mode of cultural production, it is subject to the same processes of reification and commodity fetishism as any form of popular entertainment. The social processes by which stars are fetishized and their music is tailored for mass consumption are reproduced from one realm of culture to another; the way in which Luciano Pavarotti is marketed and sold is indistinguishable from that of the Spice Girls.

The bourgeois idealization of art as a sphere of contemplation was also subject to the attacks of artists themselves. Modernist movements in the early twentieth century, Russian Constructivism and Italian Futurism in particular, sought to eliminate the boundary between art and politics as social domains. These were attempts not merely to expand the vocabulary of art to include overtly political images and content but also to recast the role and the forms of art in changing social conditions. Art had the potential not only to represent or to document new directions in politics and society but also to participate in social production (particularly in the Russian case), to legitimize political movements and to create an opening for revolutionary forms of consciousness. In both movements, art took on a vanguardist role, where new aesthetic forms as well as new possibilities of form itself became correlates to new forms of political engagement. Yet the attempts to sublate art and politics failed. While the modernist avant-gardes shared a number of principles with revolutionary politics in this period, both leninist and fascist, as forms of practice art and politics never converged (Bowler, 1992). The formal imperatives of artists making art were frequently at a variance with, and could not continue to be subordinated to, the instrumentalities of day-to-day politics. This led to increasing conflicts between artists and political leaders and, whether through disillusionment or the construction of institutional barriers, to the elimination of avant-garde artists from any formal role in political life.[1]

The foregoing examples suggest that the differentiation of art in the early modern period was far from stable. Neither was it self-evident nor adequately resolved through purely formal aesthetic considerations. As art became differentiated from church and court in Europe in the eighteenth century, it was nevertheless subject to the market. The meaning or content of art shifted within a newly contextualized social domain, both of which had to do with the increasing social power of the bourgeoisie. The sacralization of high art at the turn of century and the attempt to secure its differentiation through institutional means was a response to the democratic conditions of culture in the United States. It had the result of limiting the content and specifying the form of what was to be called art at the same time that it obscured the real embeddedness of art in other social processes. The attempt to eliminate the distinction between art and politics, which generated new forms of art in the Soviet Union and fascist Italy in the early twentieth century, occurred within a redefinition of politics that opened up new possibilities for artists in the period. Yet the specificity of art, or the persistence of its differentiation, could not be circumvented even in this most self-conscious attempt. The boundaries of the social domain of art and its internal criteria of meaning and form are mutually constituted. The identity of the social domain of art emerges simultaneously, and continuously, with its differentiation from other social domains.

The social differentiation of art in the contemporary period appears to be more openly contested than ever before, and descriptions of it are correspondingly weaker. The tendency toward a broader definition of art has developed, in more recent scholarship, into a tendency toward the elimination of the category altogether and the dedifferentiation of art as a social domain, actual social conditions notwithstanding. Leslie Fiedler's call to "Cross the Border—Close the Gap" (1977), between high art and popular culture was part of a continuing effort to criticize the institutionalization of high art in the narrow sense, with respect to criticism and reception. Certainly audience crossover was not new, although it seemed to come as a revelation that the marketing categories of the culture industry were conveniences that streamlined business more than they dictated taste. Similarly, while the curatorial or repertoire decisions of elite institutions of high culture reproduced the distinction between high art and popular culture, we have no evidence that suggests that the opera buff was not also an aficionado of swing. Critics like Fiedler and Susan Sontag (1966) became self-conscious of participating in a discursive reproduction of the high art domain, in that only high art was accorded scholarly attention. What resulted from the postmodern criticism was a broader definition of art, legitimizing more types of literature, music and visual art as art, but not, in the early period, any real question about the integrity of the domain of art itself. Comparative lists of the modern versus the postmodern, attempts to catalog the distinctions between them and to define the postmodern terrain, included a wide assortment of titles and artists under the rubric of art, without any self-consciousness about how that new category was constructed and, as Calhoun (1995: 106) has observed, without any self-consciousness about the dichotomous, modernist construction of the lists themselves (see, for example, Hassan, 1987, and Calinescu, 1987).

The postmodern critique made it clear that institutional differentiation was no longer adequate to account for the identity of the social domain of art because "art" was going on outside of those institutional parameters. Once the sacred nature of high art was dismantled, however, a broader question about social differentiation emerged. Art was not differentiated solely through formal criteria, through its institutional base or through modes of production that were distinct from those of other social products, particularly as the products of the culture industry could now also be considered art. Given this state of affairs, the field of art was open not just to popular entertainment but also to other cultural forms. The question being raised was not whether Indonesian monkey chants could properly be called music but whether advertising should be considered art. The problem of music (classical or popular) as a commodity paled in comparison to the question of whether or not graffiti is art. On what grounds could art be distinguished from fashion photographs or quilting, or could music performance be distinguished from athletic competitions, or modern dance from sex? In other words, it was not merely the internal distinctions between types of art, characteristic of aesthetic discourse since the institutional separation of high art from popular culture, that was called into question, but the parameters of the social domain of art itself.

One response, influenced by poststructuralist thought, has been to shift analysis from such problematic categories as "literature" and "painting" to broader issues of signification and language, or images and representation—that is, the underlying communicative processes and media upon which art depends. However, as the histories of Constructivism and Futurism show, their specificity as forms of *aesthetic* communication remains terribly important. What is more, social differentiation continues to structure everyday social practice regardless of how fluid the

categories and how contested the meanings. The social differentiation of art is continually being articulated in communications that reproduce the distinction between art and other forms
of social practice. For instance, we debate what is art and
whether or not a particular work is art, or in whose opinion or
in what cultural setting that work would be art. These debates
are supported by institutional arrangements that contribute to
the notion that there is something that is art that remains distinct
from other human endeavors. Even discussions about whether
or not there is a meaningful category of "art"—that is, even the
rejection of art—draw on an existing aesthetic discourse.[2] The
terms of the debate, the aesthetic categories used in analysis as
well as in everyday communication, are remarkably supple and
always provisional. It is not possible to decide, once and for all,
what art is. Nevertheless, insofar as they reproduce criteria of
meaning internal to the social domain of art, they also reproduce
its differentiation. That said, while these communications lend
the social domain of art some kind of provisional form, they do
not result in the mapping out of an agreed-upon vocabulary of
aesthetic discourse or a definitive set of aesthetic practices.[3]

This analysis is based on the form of contingency as a model
of differentiation. The important theoretical contribution of the
concept of contingency is that it recognizes form in motion and
provides the means by which theory can cope with conditions
of flux. Contingency articulates the differentiation of the social
domain of art as a process that is never finally resolved. It is not
determined by a preexisting structure, already marked off from
the rest of social reality. The boundaries of the field are in fact
elements of the field and are continually being rearticulated. At
the same time, the ongoing production of the field of art is based
on forms of internal reference—that is, criteria of meaning specific to art. These constitute a set of prior selections of differing
durations and degrees of consensus that are subject to continual
and contingent reproduction and change. Contingency describes
this dynamic form of social differentiation as flux (eventfulness
structured by selections) within limiting conditions (of internal

reference). Contingency as the form of social differentiation is continually emergent.

TEMPORALITY / THE EVENTFULNESS OF FORM

Contingency adds the temporal dimension to a notion of standpoint as a function of space. The standpoint of critique is not just a matter of position—with respect to art works, social steering mechanisms, or identity. Critique is also situated within, and contributes to, a dynamic present. Time and space are mutually implied, and any notion of standpoint must take this into account. In a dynamic social terrain, no standpoint is stationary, nor is any critique the final word. Autonomy, in the form of the negative dialectic, was used to establish a standpoint for critique at a distance from social steering mechanisms and yet within the object domain of society. Both of these are spatial designations. On the other hand, contingency situates critique within the eventfulness of the social domain of art, a designation of both time and space.

Social processes, including differentiation, are temporally complex. This means that processes are not necessarily linear and that they operate on several temporal levels. Thus far, the analysis has proceeded historically, to demonstrate how contingency grasps the two-sided character of differentiation as an ongoing process. Historical temporality is more accessible to analysis, since provisional results of the process are already available for observation. Yet in order to understand how the social domain of art functions, and therefore how critique is situated, it must be observed in its present eventfulness. The dynamics of the social domain of art are ongoing; they occur not only over time but with every event on the terrain of art. Seen in this light, historical change is merely a particularly observable (because of longer duration) set of events within an already dynamic field. Contingency as the form of social differentiation establishes the standpoint of critique in the ongoing, two-sided distinction of art from other social domains. Music will provide the illustration of how this works. The social differentiation of music can be articulated in two sets of propositions:

1. Insofar as every distinction has two sides that are mutually constitutive, reproduction is ongoing differentiation. The internal criteria of musical meaning on which musical production, in the broad sense, is based are distinct from other social domains. All new work or new communication that is based on these criteria therefore rearticulates the distinction between music and other social domains.

2. Each new event, or work, enters into a dynamic field and has the capacity to alter its boundaries. In one sense, this alteration is immediate. Insofar as any event is new, it adds something to what already exists and by definition reconfigures or restates the domain. If the event is of short duration, if the information is easily normalized, observable change is unlikely. If, on the other hand, the event is of longer duration, change becomes observable. Yet each new event calls the boundaries into question, to be reproduced or altered, whether in the moment or over time through other communicative events.

In sum, the integrity of the social domain of music is maintained in conditions of flux both through the reproduction of its meaning structures and the recurrent articulation of its boundaries. The crucial point here is that both of these processes are contingent, which means not only that they are unpredictable but more specifically that they continually emerge through a series of selections. These selections are communicative forms of practice based on meaning. Previously existing criteria of meaning do not determine selection but make selection possible, just as contingency makes selection necessary.

Musical meaning, the way music means, or the set of references that make music meaningful, are of fairly long duration. The conception of music as organized or meaningful sound is not likely to fluctuate wildly from day to day, although radical changes are always possible. Specific forms of musical organization or meaning can be of varying duration: from that of the system of tonality, which has long structured musical production in the West, to stylistic variations, like stride piano, which exist as a potential, as part of the available repertoire of meaning, but are not necessarily actualized in the present. Yet music as a social domain is also eventful in that every new musical work enters into an existing field of reference and generates new communication about music.[4] To the extent that most new music is made to conform with already existing meaning structures, the field can absorb or normalize a great deal of new information. However, some work cannot be so easily normalized, and it reconfigures the terrain in unpredictable ways.

Rap is a good contemporary example of this process. It has changed the terrain of music in that, first, both melody and harmony are subordinated to the rhythm of words; second, sampling and other production techniques that employ already existing musical material challenge conventional notions of authenticity and hence of value. In rap, rhyme and meter substitute for conventional popular song form. Junctures or breaks in the music are indicated by the juxtaposition of tape loops rather than by musical bridges. These tape loops usually consist of material sampled from existing recordings and environments and are used as rhythmic background. What is new about rap is not just content (what rappers are talking about) or attitude (the way they are talking about it), but forms of musical meaning.

The use of found objects was arguably a condition of production—tape loops and rhythmic effects that are the basic tracks for rappers could be produced with home stereos and eliminated the need for traditional instruments like bass and drums. However, appropriation of this sort has had aesthetic, economic, technological and legal consequences. As an aesthetic matter, any notion of the musical product being commensurate with an original composition has been superseded by the originality of production. In addition, issues of copyright and ownership, legal matters with important economic consequences, have become immensely complicated and, as more and more lawyers are needed to disentangle competing claims, have shifted the terrain between music and the legal system.

Rap has also generated numerous other legal challenges, given the violence and obscenity issues, and some of these incidents have fueled political debate regarding regulation of the entertainment industry. Rap was, at least before its commercialization, based on the image rappers have of themselves, rather than something that was manufactured for them or polished to fit industry norms. The rawness, and in some cases untempered hostility, of both the image and the words raised questions of whether rap was legitimating the real experiences of ghetto kids or glamorizing violence, misogyny, and anti-Semitism. The politics of rap have always been at issue. In addition, the violence—both portrayed in music and actually lived—and obscenity of rap lyrics have made rap the subject of more legal challenges than any other type of music. CDs have been pulled from stores, concerts have been canceled, and rappers have frequently appeared in court (Williams-Crenshaw, 1997; Dubin, 1992). The social domain of music continues to respond to rap as a series of events that have reconfigured its terrain. Yet even though rap has made the relations between music and other social domains more complex, even though some of its forms of musical reference are new, rap has been legitimized with its own category at the Grammy Awards and a very respectable profit margin for the recording industry. In other words, rap has not changed the identity of music as music, but constitutes a contingent articulation of its difference.

On the other hand, it is unlikely that the current "explosion" of Latin music will have anything like the same effect, both within the field of musical reference or with respect to other social domains. Latin is the currently, or recurrently, hip exotica. Within the field of music criticism, it has generated much the same commentary that it did ten years ago. A full-page story in the Sunday *New York Times* of January 4, 1998, ostensibly about Paul Simon's and Buster Poindexter's appropriations of Latin music, featured a half-page photo of Carmen Miranda. Unlike rap, Latin music fills the role of "the other"—in this case, an unambiguously feminized other.[5] In its recurrence as an aspect of the music scene, the value of Latin music lies in its perceived authenticity, in conforming to conventional notions of what Latin music should sound like, rather than as a possible source of anything new. Although there are, and always have been, musics in which Latin forms are used to innovate or to invent a new musical vocabulary, this is not the basis on which Latin music is recurrently popularized. Despite the many types of crossover, its basic forms and meaning structures have not changed. Even the current configuration, designed to attract a younger Latin audience, is better described as *nuevo salsa* with a hiphop attitude rather than as anything new.[6] What is more, the Latin explosion is not an indicator of broader social ramifications; Puerto Ricans haven't gained more social status, Cubans are not defining themselves in new ways with respect to mainstream American culture. The record companies expect that Cuba will open up as a market with the anticipated end of Castro, but that does nothing to alter the boundaries of the musical field itself. Even if it's in Cuba, it's still business as usual.

Like rap, the Latin phenomenon arose and is occurring through a series of contingent selections within the domain of music. There is no particular logic to the fact that the record industry chose to produce rap when it did, nor is there a particular logic to its popularity. Rap had been around for fifteen years before the major labels started buying it, and it would have been impossible to predict that the biggest audience for it would be suburban white kids. In the case of Latin music, the factors that contribute to its recurrence are even more serendipitous; it seems that jazz or rock composers use it as a resource when they need to hear something new, and then abandon it when it has served its limited purpose. This is not to suggest that there are no reasons behind these phenomena, or that the reasons elude analysis. The recurrence of "authentic" Latin music and the production and popularity of rap are not arbitrary. There are contributing factors that can be identified, such as, in the case of rap, impending competition from independent labels. Their actualization is nevertheless contingent; reasons do not necessarily add up to an overriding rationality in which any specific course of events appears as necessary. The field of music is continually being generated through events with different temporal structures. Some, like rap, may be of longer duration, given that the new information takes longer to normalize and presents more challenges to the integrity of the field. Others, like Latin music, are recurring phenomena, although every recurrence is also new because it occurs within a different context. Other events may merely dissipate and some, like nostalgia for oldies, appear to function in reverse. Moreover, all of these phenomena or events occur at the same time as the reproduction of high art or classical music by symphony orchestras and string quartets, as well as in a variety of highly publicized competitions for young virtuosos. There is no way to know which events will be more global, which more local in their effects, which of longer or shorter duration. They are contingent and could always have turned out otherwise. Rap could have hit a wall of criticism that scared off the record companies, keeping it a more local phenomenon, just as its forms of musical innovation might never have been used by other musicians to enlarge the frame of musical reference. These specific occurrences are a function of day-to-day selections in the ongoing production of new work and new communication about music, all of which occur with reference to the other side of the distinction—that is, other social domains.

The concept of contingent differentiation has utility not only as a description of how the social domain of music actually functions but also for reconsidering the standpoint of critique. Critique is both situated in and contributes to this eventfulness. It does not occur against an unchanging backdrop of aesthetic norms from which its categories can be derived, or in the context of modes of cultural production that function primarily as social reproduction. Critique is situated not just in space but in time, and the advantage of this model is that it becomes clear that the two are mutually implied. Critique does not occur within a space carved out of space or as a moment in time out of time. It is embedded in both historical and present temporality and situated within a social domain that is continually emergent.

The foregoing commentary on rap and Latin music is the beginning of a critique based on the form of contingency, one that looks at both internal and external forms of reference and is situated within an eventful present.[7] The critique takes place on the terrain of music but recognizes that it is a terrain that is in flux, as its differentiation from other social domains is ongoing. Furthermore, the events it observes are contingent rather than necessary, emergent rather than fixed, and critique itself is subject to the same contingency. It cannot take refuge in the universal or the particular, in transcendent or immanent positions, or in a fixed identity or subject position. A temporalized structure of critique, based on the form of contingency, resolves the problem of reification and is consistent with actual social conditions. What it gives up is the comfort, or the pretense, of being either final or fixed, which has been its singular weakness.

Events that contribute to the ongoing differentiation of the social domain of music are not simply those made by musicians or in the medium of music, as is clear from the examples above. They are also the communications about music generated by new work. This includes what is said publicly about music in criticism, on the radio, and in academic journals; what the record industry, fanzines, clubs, and philharmonic societies present as music; as well as the ongoing practices of buying records, going to concerts, listening to the radio, and private conversations, which are communicative to varying degrees.[8] All of these contribute to the ongoing production of the social domain of music and its continual differentiation from other social domains. The process is both bottom up and top down, neither overdetermined nor completely random.

CONTINGENCY / THE STRUCTURE OF CRITIQUE

Although critique has been construed, and often conducted, as the rigid application of pregiven aesthetic standards, the critical theorists recognized that critique arises out of instability, out of a tension between possibilities that can only provisionally be resolved. Autonomy, in the form of the negative dialectic, was a principle of contingency in that it was neither necessary nor impossible. Autonomy established a distance between art and social steering mechanisms that was unstable and therefore had continually to be either reclaimed or reevaluated. The theoretical problem has been to retain this dynamic element in critique and analysis—in other words, to provide some grounds for critique without reifying the very thing that gives it life. Contingency accomplishes this by situating critique within a dynamic present, a present marked by the continual distinction of art from other social domains. In the process, it also provides an alternative to the universalist position, outside of time, or the particularist one, without meaningful social context.

Autonomy as the basic form of aesthetic critique became inadequate, not because it is no longer valid to make distinctions but because its form became reified. The full implications of its contingency, of being based on a tension that could never be resolved or of a status that continually had to be marked out, became incompatible with the need to establish a foothold for critique within the totalizing conditions of Enlightenment reason. If we no longer think of reason as totalizing, if the conditions of knowledge have changed or our description of them has become more complex, then the conditions in which critique is situated have also changed. The implications of the postmodern understanding of knowledge as fragmented, local, or fluid have to be addressed. However, far from the death knell of critique, these conditions present an opportunity to reconfigure the dynamic character of critique that the Frankfurt School theorists were forced to abandon. If the structure of knowledge is more dynamic, it is also more compatible with dynamic forms of critique.

Yet just as contingency often drops out of systematic theory, it has been viewed as similarly incompatible with critique. The forms in which critique has been conducted through the modern period suggest that the project of critique is to generate universally valid statements, or to make distinctions between artworks or cultural practices based on criteria that have general validity. By this articulation, it would not be possible to take contingency, which implies both selection and risk, into account. However, contingency and critique are not mutually exclusive, any more than contingency is incompatible with general theory. Aesthetic critique is a process of making distinctions that both depends upon and discloses contingency. Critique arises out of contingency, for if matters are settled once and for all, if events proceed out of necessity, then taking a position becomes irrelevant. Critique is a form of action, and action can occur only if there is freedom to act. Critique also discloses contingency in that it is never an end result or a final verdict; rather it is a moment in a process that generates more critique. Therefore, the position that emerges as its form is always a contingent one, subject to further elaboration, communication or disputation.

The model of contingency developed here incorporates freedom in that it is premised on selection, and temporality, in that it is ongoing. The importance of temporality to critique was a significant finding in a study of music criticism I conducted in New York City in 1985 (Hanrahan, 1993). The study addressed the question of why there was so little real criticism of jazz, in the form of considered judgments, despite the growing number of publications that devoted space to writing about jazz, including *The New York Times*. In a series of in-depth interviews, jazz writers cited the format considerations of publications, which, because they are likely to be short, do not allow for extended discussion and are more suited to reporting or to the snappy review. They discussed the need to legitimize jazz as a subject of critique, which inclines writers to be less critical. Most important, they suggested that the critical voice or position only develops over time. It is through the process of continually making distinctions, making judgments about jazz, seeing them in print and having the opportunity to refine or reevaluate them as part of an ongoing discussion with other writers, that a critical voice comes into being. Given the occupational constraints on most writers, the vast majority of whom are freelance, the opportunities to develop that voice are extremely rare. Most writers spend so much time just trying to get into print and, in the constant effort to sell their work, to conform to the style of whatever publication they are pitching, that fragmentation is the norm. In their own words, much of what they write is not critique or even criticism but merely reporting in that it does not involve any self-disclosure. The findings of the study suggest that critique will become even more rare if the tendencies of the publishing industry to move away from staff positions and long-term employment go unchecked.

Critique is contingent not only in that it is a moment in a process, generating more critique, but also because position is continually emergent. It is generated in the process of making distinctions—that is, in the process of critique itself. Position is not a fixed category, such as *woman, marxist,* or *sociologist,* but something that emerges continually over time. Critique that assumes a position and hence a form as a priori is not critique in any real sense of the term but is a type of ideological reproduction, insofar as it reproduces and reifies distinctions that have already been made. Orthodoxy is, by definition, static.

CONCLUSION

According to Hannah Arendt ([1954] 1977b: 243), contingency is inherent in the realm of politics in that it is the corollary of freedom. The fact that things could always have turned out otherwise is the price that human beings pay for their freedom to act in the political realm. Yet far from making politics meaningless, the fact that action is open-ended and its outcomes are unknown lends an urgency to political judgment and presents opportunities for individual distinction. Arendt (1958) conceives of democratic politics as a specific type of action, a process in which, among equals, the speaker distinguishes or discloses herself. To think and act politically is not merely to assert one's private opinion but to engage in what Arendt ([1954] 1977a) calls representative thinking, to think from the point of view of others, to take others into account in forming judgments. This is crucial because "The power of judgment rests on a potential agreement with others" (220), and only by this means is persuasion possible and does disclosure serve a distinctly political function. The contingency of action or of human affairs is not, then, grounds for relativism, but implies a unique type of responsibility for acting and speaking in the presence of others.

The notion of judgment is also linked to contingency in that judgment in the political realm cannot be based on claims to rational truth. Unlike, for instance, mathematical truths, there is no absolute right or wrong that transcends the realm of human affairs. Political forms of judgment can only be based on factual truth, on events witnessed and agreed upon by the many. Interestingly, Kant (whose *Critique of Judgment* is central to Arendt's argument) arrived at the notion that the faculty of judgment is a political one when he was examining the phenomenon of taste; that is, with respect to aesthetic matters (221):

Culture and politics, then, belong together because it is not knowledge or truth which is at stake, but rather judgment and decision, the judicious exchange of opinion about the sphere of public life and the common world. (223)

To the extent that art and politics share the public space, they are linked by the faculty of judgment.

Contingency is a condition of politics as well as of critique. Aesthetic critique is a process of persuasion and judgment that distinguishes the speaker and, because it is always ambiguous with regard to truth, also discloses contingency. Aesthetic critique is also political in that it speaks to the conditions of public life and takes others into account. The contingency of aesthetic categories and meaning do not vitiate judgment or lead to a type of relativism that makes judgment impossible. On the contrary, contingency is the precondition of judgment in both politics and art.

NOTES

1. Although the aesthetic production of groups like the Futurists were at odds with the regime's attempt to create a monumental fascist art, as Mabel Berezin (1997) points out, the performing arts continued to play an important role in fascist Italy.

2. It is worth noting in this regard that the attempt in cultural studies to do without the category of art as an elite construction has resulted in both serious analysis of the objects and practices of popular culture and the elimination of art and aesthetic questions from the field as a whole. Hunter (1992) and Wolff (1992) have both spoken to this problem.

3. Nor do they map out a field of objectively determined relations. Among contemporary theorists, Pierre Bourdieu (1984, 1993, 1996) has devoted serious attention to social differentiation and the constitution of specific fields, such as art. According to Bourdieu, the field of cultural production is a realm of self-interest and acquisition, driven by a distinct form of capital—cultural capital. It is homologous to the field of economic production in that the same objective relations obtain in both fields and those relations are economically determined. However, the homologous construction of Bourdieu's argument is reductive and obscures the complexity of the cultural field. Bourdieu suggests that what is specific about the cultural field is its "disavowal of the economic," the presumption that something other than crass economic interest drives the pursuit of cultural capital. He is indeed correct in suggesting that the criterion of real value in cultural goods is often the appearance of unsalability, a point that Adorno ([1938] 1982) had made much earlier (Horkheimer and Adorno, [1944] 1972). Yet the difference between art and the economic field is far more complex than a simple "no" to the economic "yes"; a "bad faith economy" as opposed to a genuine one. Aesthetic criteria of meaning, expressivity and communication, as well as aesthetic forms themselves, are not engaged in Bourdieu's argument. What is more, this formulation does not take into account other forms of reference and meaning that differentiate art from the legal system,

science, religion or politics. In other words, art has multiple system relations and therefore its forms of distinction are more complex than a homology to the economy allows.

4. Bourdieu entertains one aspect of this phenomenon in his analysis of the cultural field. He writes, "To introduce difference is to produce time" (1993: 106). What Bourdieu suggests is that the history of the field, its temporal structure, if you will, is redefined with every new artist and trend. As new works appear, the classics may be either invoked or rejected, changing their historical status, and what was just recently defined as contemporary floats in a kind of limbo until its place in the field is reestablished. My work elaborates on this in suggesting that not only is each difference an event within the system, but each event has the capacity to alter the boundaries of the system itself. It is an argument situated within a broader conception of social differentiation and premised on the notion that the cultural field both has multiple references to other social systems and is continually emergent.

5. Not that the music itself is not often macho, but it is consistently treated as a sensuous alternative to the more square and predictable rhythms of conventional pop music.

6. I have Kip Hanrahan to thank for this particular insight and for important contributions to my understanding of rap.

7. It is only the beginning of a critique in that it demonstrates how the form of contingency situates critique, but it does not address evaluative questions. This will be taken up in Chapter 5.

8. I am in broad agreement with Bourdieu's (1993: 110) notion that "discourse about a work is not mere accompaniment, intended to assist its perception and appreciation, but a stage in the production of the work, of its meaning and value." The elaboration here is that these discursive or communicative events are not only productive of the work but also constitute the system as a whole through reproducing the distinction between music and other social domains.

3

SYSTEM

Contingency is central to the context of critique as the form of social differentiation, yet the notion of music as a differentiated social domain remains to be elaborated. In addition, basic categories in the sociology of music, such as meaning, production and the work of art, must be reformulated to make them compatible with this context and more suitable for cultural analysis and critique.

To begin, music is a functionally differentiated social subsystem that uses communication as a mode of reproduction and in which meaning functions both as premise and as the capacity for managing contingency in system operations.[1] Formulating a critical sociology of music within the framework of systems theory offers the advantages of allowing for the differentiation of social domains as autonomy within society, and for contingency as a description of social processes. It also makes it possible to conceive of meaningful critiques based on temporal differentiation, to be discussed in Chapter 4. In these crucial respects, the theory of open systems proves to be a more useful model than others that commonly inform the sociology of culture—including the closed systems theories of the last generation.

MUSIC AS A SOCIAL SUBSYSTEM

In contemporary work in systems theory, the distinction between closed and open systems indicates an important conceptual shift. Physicists agree that closed systems, though still existent, form only a small part of the physical universe. Most phenomena of interest are in fact open systems, exchanging energy, matter or information with their environments. Intuitively, the concept of open systems makes even more sense with respect to social systems, given the contingency of human experience, action and decision. Social systems are constantly undergoing change and dissolution, in addition to integration, maintenance and reproduction, and they always include an element of unpredictability. Given the dynamic nature of human life, a closed social system can exist only under extraordinary conditions and for a brief period of time (as would any physical system in a state of equilibrium) or as a theoretical abstraction.

Aspects of these ideas are already present in George Herbert Mead's ([1932] 1959) effort to base new concepts of sociality on contemporary advances in relativity theory.[2] In contemporary sociology, Niklas Luhmann has developed the most sophisticated model of a theory of open systems. The theory takes as a premise that, in modern conditions, society has become sufficiently differentiated to produce autopoietic (self-reproducing) and self-referential subsystems. Art—like politics, the economy and science, among others—is such a subsystem. In addition, there are subsystems of subsystems; for example, music is a subsystem of the subsystem of art; sociology is a subsystem of the subsystem of science, and so on. The basic elements of these subsystems are communications—a subsystem reproduces itself to the extent that it continues to generate communication. In addition, meaningful communications within subsystems are self-referential, which is to say that music is meaningful as music only within the subsystem of music. Within the subsystem of the economy, it's a product or a commodity; within the legal system, it's intellectual property; within the political system, it's a form of legitimation or dissent. In this conceptualization, music is a social subsystem that is open with respect to the environment but closed with respect to meaning.

Social systems are dynamic in a dual sense. System identity is a process of ongoing distinction from the environment, and at the same time, systems generate their own components as dynamic elements of the system. Given that eventfulness is inherent in the system, the question of system identity—*what* is the social domain of music—becomes the question of *how* it functions. As a consequence, sociological analysis is structured around system operations of autopoiesis, the process of ongoing production of elements that reproduce the system/environment distinction; and both resonance and translation, which explain system relations with other social systems.[3] Among the implications for sociological analysis of music are the following. First, social processes of production and reception are repositioned within the dynamic context of system operations. The conventional sociological coding of these processes is altered, insofar as they are not discrete but rather simultaneous aspects of communicative reproduction. In addition, all of the components of the social system of music are themselves dynamic, which reconfigures the central category of musical work. Third, analysis turns on a sociological concept of meaning as the means through which system operations are accomplished. Finally, these conceptual shifts present different possibilities for articulating the social function of music and addressing the question of its autonomy.

AUTOPOIESIS

The example of rap demonstrates how the integrity of the social domain of music is maintained in conditions of flux, both through the reproduction of its meaning structures and the recurrent articulation of its boundaries. In the theory of open systems, autopoiesis is the process that describes the ongoing production, as contingent reproduction, of any social system in distinction from its environment. Autopoietic systems are not only self-organizing, producing and eventually changing their own structures, they are also self-constituting, producing all of the components used by the system that recursively constitute the system (Luhmann, 1990: 3). In this way autopoietic systems achieve self-referential closure. Even the boundaries of the system "are components of the system and cannot be taken as given by a preconstituted world" (Luhmann, 1990: 7).

Although Luhmann's work is descended from Talcott Parsons, the theoretical shift from self-referential structural integration to self-referential constitution of elements substantively alters the basic concept of system maintenance.

Maintenance is not simply a question of replication, of cultural transmission, of reproducing the *same patterns* under similar circumstances, e.g., using forks and knives while eating and only while eating, but the primary process is the production of *next elements* in the actual situation, *and these have to be different from the previous one* to be recognizable as events. This does not exclude the relevance of preservable patterns; it even requires them for a sufficient quick recognition of next possibilities. However, the system maintains itself not by storing patterns but by producing elements, not by transmitting *memes* (units of cultural transmission analogue to *genes*) but by recursively using events for producing events. (Luhmann, 1990: 9)

Autopoietic social systems are dynamic in the most fundamental sense: they use events to produce events. These events are understood as communications, which for Luhmann are the basic elements of all social systems. As events, communications cannot be accumulated, for it is in the nature of events to pass. But their dissolution is a necessary cause of reproduction. In a system that is maintained as a system only by continually producing its own elements, as events pass, more events must be generated. Moreover, in such a dynamic system, reproduction is never the unmodified return of what has already been, but rather the production of what comes next. In a radical conceptual shift, it is therefore the *instability* of its elements that is a condition of the system's duration rather than the stability. Far from a static concept of system integration, "time and irreversibility are built into the system not only at the structural level but also at the level of its elements" (Luhmann, 1990: 10). This is a very musical concept. Music's evanescence—its passing, its temporality—has often been considered an instability impossible to theorize. However, this temporality is a constitutive aspect of the theory of open systems. Music is eventful in that it consists of communicative events that generate other events and because its temporality necessitates ongoing reproduction. As musical events (or sounds) pass, others must be generated in order for music to continue. Music progresses, and therefore exists, only through the contingent production of meaningful musical elements. It is stability, rather than instability, that threatens the system's duration. In musical terms, stability is silence, or the end of music as music.

Autopoietic systems are paradoxical, functioning despite an element of arbitrariness in decisions, unpredictability in action and confusion in communication. Communicative events are not necessarily rational, nor do misunderstanding and rejection shut down autopoiesis. The inherent ambiguities of aesthetic communication provide perhaps the best case in point. Debates over what music means, the seeming arbitrariness of aesthetic or musical preferences, and even the outright rejection of music all constitute part of the ongoing reproduction of the social subsystem of music. Even conflict is not the end of autopoiesis but the precipitation of a change of state. The autopoiesis of social systems "does not stop in the face of logical contradictions" (Luhmann, 1990: 8).

However, while communication is not necessarily rationally grounded, neither is it arbitrary. The system is always processing information and making selections in autopoietic reproduction, and these selections are based on meaning. The shift from rational to paradoxical systems is not the shift, in postmodern theory, from meaning to meaninglessness or from order to randomness. On the contrary, meaning is everywhere as a precondition of selection and is constantly being generated by the process of selection. Debates about what art means always depend on available meanings; even rejection is based on expectations generated within the system of meaning. Yet in neither case does existing meaning determine the outcome. If meaning did not exist, there would be no basis on which to make selections, but it is always being constituted by the process of selection. Meaning-based selection both reduces complexity and preserves it, in that the options not selected remain options. The negation that is a correlative of selection is provisional; meaning is never decided once and for all.

Communications, defined as syntheses of information, utterance and understanding (including misunderstanding) (Luhmann, 1990: 3), are produced and make sense within that system's frame of self-reference. Communications meaningful within the subsystem of music take place both in the medium of music and in communication about music. They take the form of utterances or talking about music, written criticism, making music, performance, listening to music, and so on. All of these communications are understood as events that guarantee that the system will be able to continue to reproduce itself. None are privileged. Whether about the fine points of 12-tone composition or the type of amplifier the guitarist used, communications ensure the ongoing self-reproduction of the subsystem of music. In other words, the self-reference of meaning constitutes a limiting condition, with respect not to the legitimacy of specific musical forms but to the meaningful content of communication. Within the subsystem of music, it doesn't make sense to discuss the principles of aerodynamics with respect to 12-tone composition, or to compare the amplifier to a crate of bananas. Communication is contingent but not random; it functions in autopoietic reproduction to reproduce the system/environment distinction.

The model of communication occurring and making sense within a network of communications is also particularly well suited to musical work. Once music becomes available as music through performance—live or recorded—it is communicative in an expressive sense in which the contingency of reception is preserved. This constitutes a shift away from intersubjective models of aesthetic communication developed by second-generation critical theorists, notably Albrecht Wellmer (1984). Just as Habermas (1984) had developed the notion of communicative rationality as an alternative to more instrumental forms, Wellmer used intersubjective communication as an alternative to Adorno's concepts of expert listening and commodity listening, which subordinated the listener to the work and to the culture industry, respectively. However, music is not language, and performance is not a conversation. Live performance may have an intersubjective dimension in instances in which music is improvised and performed in intimate settings, but these instances are highly unusual. The more general tendency is toward modeling live performance on technological reproduction, with lip-synching to prerecorded music and dressing to match the video clips in stadium-size arenas only the most extreme forms. In these cases, each listener may hear or respond to the music in more or less individual ways, but there is no possibility of the audience shaping the musical outcome. A systems conception of communication accounts for the open-ended character of musical reception without premising it on idealizations of either performance or reception.

Communication also effectively grounds the notion of music as social practice. It provides an elaboration of Stuart Hall's definition of culture as signifying practice, the product of which is meaning (1980: 30) by situating it within social limiting conditions. Practice is not free-floating; communication functions in system reproduction and is based on existing meaning systems at the same time that it continually generates new meaning.

Finally, the theory of open systems also overturns the Parsonian idea that music or art is a societal subsystem of pattern maintenance, communicating affective values and norms of society and contributing to the maintenance of the social order. Rather, in a dynamic model of ongoing and yet contingent reproduction, art is a social system that is maintained only through the continual production and dissolution of communicative events. These are generated with respect to existing meaning, and they continually produce new meaning. Given that internal forms of reference are the premise of meaningful communications, ongoing and contingent production of communications reproduces the distinction between system and environment that is constitutive of system identity.

MUSICAL WORK

Contingency renders the object as flux within limiting conditions, and this applies to the category of musical work. Artworks are theoretically significant in systems theory, not as formally constructed aesthetic objects but as programs for communications about themselves. Without musical work there could be no communication about music. At the same time, the work serves to organize communications about itself, establishing limiting conditions for the communications it generates. Within the framework of system operations, musical work is an event, a crucial juncture in an ongoing communicative process. Reconceptualized in this manner, the term *musical work* applies to any genre of music, all of which function similarly in system reproduction. Further, musical work is not created as a stable or transcendent essence but in order to generate more communication. The object is both in flux and subject to contingency as it is produced and reproduced through communications. Yet its contingency is not absolute; its sounds are not chaos, and communication about them is situated within a self-referential system of meaning.

This represents an important shift from an aesthetic to a sociological definition of musical work. The conventional sociological project in music proceeded largely as an attempt to map sociological categories onto aesthetic ones, frequently in the form of homologies between aesthetic form and social structure (Weber, 1958; Adorno, 1948, 1973), distinctions between social groups and musical genres (Gans, 1974), and so on. It was a series of attempts to base what is social about music within the work, and then to translate from aesthetic to sociological categories. Other efforts in the sociology of music have sidestepped this problem by designating what is social about music as its reception or production, rather than the work itself (Peterson, 1976; Bourdieu, 1984; Wolff, 1981). Just as no homology can account for the social complexity of music, neither is it adequate for sociological analysis to relegate musical work to the purely aesthetic.

As it is reconceptualized here, musical work is social. However, what is social about music is not something formally inscribed (and therefore waiting to be read) in the work, or the ways in which the work is mediated by social processes of production, transmission and consumption. Nor is music some type of social ordering principle. Music becomes social reality insofar as it generates communication; to the extent that it generates communication meaningful only within the field of its own self-reference, it functions as a social subsystem with respect to society as a whole. This does not deny that music is art and can be analyzed in aesthetic terms, only that an aesthetic conception does not provide the basis of sociological analysis. Similarly, it does not deny the social nature of production and reception, but rather establishes music as a "social product" in a much more sophisticated sense. Sociality is not simply a question of material production but is embedded in the very notion of the work; the concept of production is extended beyond material circumstances to include all communicative events through which music is reproduced. If music is in fact constantly being generated through communications, then all communications are "production."

Within the framework of the theory of open systems, musical work is music in performance. Postmodern aesthetics has dismantled the notion of the stable aesthetic object; it is no longer possible to consider artworks as fixed or static essences, repositories of meaning or the sum of their formal characteristics. However, the musical object is unstable in a far more elemental sense. Music's material is sound, a physical phenomenon that must be immediately perceived to be sensible and which dissipates over time. Regardless of the status of music as composition, it is only actualized as music in performance. A written score is not music any more than a CD is—both must be performed, that is, reproduced as sound, in order to be music. It is sound that most distinguishes one performer or composer from another, rather than the formal elements of their music. That is why attempts in jazz to resurrect "the music" of Thelonius Monk or Charles Mingus in special tribute bands serve only to remind us that with their passing, the essential element of that music is gone forever. Similarly, a Bob Dylan song or an Astor Piazzolla composition is indistinguishable from the composer's specific performance of it. Again, whether the music is substantially improvised, as in the case of jazz, or thoroughly composed, as is Piazzolla's, it is the sound that identifies the music.

Reception is implicit in the notion of musical work as performance. Yet listening is not a pure state of concentration or absorption but an aspect of present experience, subject to both temporal disjunction and the frame of a situation. Even with a brand new CD, one has no guarantee of attaining a pure and uninterrupted state of listening. Not only does the phone ring or one's attention wander; reception is rarely so pure that one can avoid bringing into the moment of listening random thoughts, specific associations and prior expectations not strictly a product of the music. Similarly, listening alone or with others at a party, a concert, or while dancing will all structure responses and expectations differently. Reception therefore continually alters the boundaries of the object itself; those elements that structure reception are not part of the music per se but constitute an aspect of what is actually heard. Reception is a situated event, neither a pure form of consciousness nor a form of intersubjective communication.

The eventfulness of musical work is twofold, both in its performance and as an aspect of system operations. Yet in neither case is this eventfulness open-ended. The temporality of music as performance is structured, to one degree or another, through the specific presentation of musical elements. Further, just as every musical sound is an event situated within performance, performance is an event situated within a dynamic system of communications and contributes to the autopoiesis of the system. In this framework, production and reception are not discrete and sequential processes but rather simultaneous moments of the work. Finally, the shift from an aesthetic to a sociological conception of musical work relieves sociological analysis of its reliance on hierarchical aesthetic categories as well as the unfortunate bifurcation of the analysis of classical and popular musics along totally different lines. Situated within the context of system operations—that is, within a specific conceptualization of society rather than a given aesthetic discourse—all music has a social function, all music functions meaningfully as music in generating communication. This is not a reductive formulation; communications about different types of music will certainly differ, will actualize a different potential of meaning within the system. The specificity of musical forms is retained at the level of situated analysis rather than functioning as a structural premise of general theory.

MEANING

If the autopoiesis of social systems is based on meaning, if social systems are in fact meaning-constituting systems; meaning emerges as a foundational sociological concept (Luhmann, 1990: Chapter 2). The concept of meaning as a system function is consistent with the contingency of musical objects as communicative events. If musical work is subject to ongoing production through contingent communication, if the work itself is continually in flux, then conventional aesthetic notions of meaning as a stable set of aesthetic references or a content embedded in the work are clearly unsatisfactory. As a sociological concept, meaning functions in the ongoing constitution of experience in its social dimension, that is, in the continual processing of communication.

Meaning "relieves consciousness of the burden of starting from zero, of having to think through all the possibilities" (Luhmann, 1990: 50). If meaning did not exist, there would be no basis on which to make selections, yet meaning is never determinant. Meaning is the premise of communication, but selection is always contingent. Meaning is a selective relationship between the actual and the potential, between the contingency of selection and the possibilities of experience that are not being actualized at that moment.

A temporalized concept of meaning as function is unusually suited to music and is the basis of the strong affinity between music and systems theory. It is not merely that music provides the best illustration of the theory, but also that systems theory provides the best analytical description of the temporalized character of musical meaning. It does so in two respects. First, the question it poses is not *what*, but *how*, does music mean? Second, it demonstrates the emergence of structure, or of temporal ordering, as a consequence of meaning-based selection. Listening is an instance par excellence of the constitution of present experience through meaning-based selection. Music is dynamic; it makes sense or is meaningful only as process. In the process of listening, we make selections about what things mean, or about which musical phenomena are important to the meaning or sense of what we're listening to. These selections then become the basis for future selections, yet they are provisional; they always stand to be revised in light of new information. In this way, structure is continually emergent; the "logic" of the piece takes shape as the constitution of experience is ongoing. Yet unlike other phenomenological models that have either been based on music (Husserl, [1964] 1991) or used to explain musical meaning (Meyer, 1956), systems theory leaves open the possibility that coherence will not be achieved, that structure is emergent but may never finally emerge, that we can end up muddled and disordered as well. In addition, listening is not always pure concentration on musical material or a particular state of consciousness, but rather, as described above, a situated event.

According to Luhmann, meaning has social, temporal and material dimensions, and this applies to musical meaning as well. Meaning is social in that it is based on some kind of consensus, it is temporal in that it has duration but is subject to change, and in the case of music its material is sound. All of these dimensions can be demonstrated as aspects of musical style. Style or genre functions as a mediating category between the uniqueness of the particular work and the conformity with existing meaning structures that ensures its communicability within the system. With respect to listening, familiarity with style preadapts certain selections based on previous patterns of actualization, yet these selections remain contingent. The use of genre as a basis for sociological analysis has been problematic for reasons that become clear in this context. As an aesthetic category, genre identifies the specific features or musical elements that are typically used in different types of musical composition or performance. As a sociological category, it is no longer a collection of concrete elements but a function, a means of both ensuring communicability and facilitating experience processing that is nevertheless always provisional and open to surprise. This more temporalized conception works against the ghettoizing tendency of genre-based sociological analysis and its reliance on deeply problematic notions of authenticity. Genre as a set of formal criteria and authenticity as a claim to its integrity have frequently been deployed to ensure that, for instance, Latin music is Latin in a clearly identifiable sense and not innovative in ways that might challenge our conceptions of "Latinness"; in other words, both genre and authenticity as aesthetic categories are static and refer to origination. As sociological categories, they refer to what is actually occurring in time. This neither constrains musical development nor relegates particular musical forms to their respective ghettos.[4]

The character of musical meaning as process, as ongoing constitution, is what is grasped by the concept of meaning as function in systems theory. For example, it doesn't make sense to say that a chord progression means something specific. It may make sense to the listener in a particular context, have a predictive quality, help to articulate the form, or to establish the song within a genre. It may appear to be predetermined if used in a particular form (like a 2-5-1 blues progression), but musical phenomena—and here it is important to understand musical elements in their dynamic sense *as* phenomena—do not mean something concrete. Rather, they function meaningfully as communication.

Meaning systems or networks of meaning are the premise for selections which, because they are always contingent, never eliminate any option absolutely. The function of meaning does not lie in arriving at a single or correct piece of information that would eliminate both a (system-relative) state of uncertainty about the world and all of its unselected possibilities.

Rather, what is special about the meaningful or meaning-based processing of experience is that it makes possible *both* the reduction and the preservation of complexity; i.e., it provides a form of selection that prevents the world from shrinking down to just one particular content of consciousness with each act of determining experience. (Luhmann, 1990: 27)

The negation upon which both selection and meaning are based is provisional. Other options do not disappear altogether but are preserved as options and remain accessible to experience.

TRANSLATION / RESONANCE

Social systems are autopoietic and self-referential, but they are not entirely self-contained. As systems that are open with respect to the environment, they are sensitive to communicative events occurring within other subsystems and able to read those communications as meaningful information. The interrelation between or interpenetration of social systems is generally understood to be an aspect of the increasing complexity of modern or postmodern societies, or at least of our descriptions of them. Yet there is some ambivalence in Luhmann's work about how to account for it. He has moved from a mechanistic input/output model of information processing (1982) to the concept of resonance (1989), to an autopoietic model in which interrelations between functionally differentiated subsystems do not appear to be analytically significant (1990). However, system relations with other subsystems are particularly important in the case of art and music, where functional differentiation is neither as complete nor as successful as it has been for other systems.[5] Nowhere is this state of affairs more evident than in the case of musical production. Luhmann's notion of resonance between social systems can be retained as a useful structuring principle with respect to the reception context of music. However, in order to explain musical production, resonance must be supplemented with another system operation that accounts for actualization. That operation, which will be referred to as *translation*, constitutes a new elaboration of the theory of open systems.

Musical production is contingent in a dual sense. First, it is highly diversified. The technology is no longer concentrated in the hands of large corporations, nor does it require intensive capitalization. Second, each production process is itself nonlinear, with a highly specific actualization. For all their obvious musical similarities, rarely do two pop songs have the same history or are two jazz albums the result of identical production processes. There is no single model of musical production, even within a particular genre of music, and there are no guarantees. However, the tendencies in cultural sociology either to reduce this complexity to a streamlined notion of musical production as a function of the economy, or to abandon any general analysis in favor of the particular, can and should be circumvented. Production as a contingent process can be described.

Any specific process of musical production is a nonrepeatable series of discrete events. This obtains regardless of whether or not the musical work produced is materially encoded in a CD, whether production is the reproduction of a written composition or spontaneously improvised in live performance. Even in the case of the production of hit songs, where the music itself is driven by existing musical formulas and the production process is highly rationalized, production is unpredictable in that it responds to unforeseen circumstances. As anyone in the business knows, just getting a record company executive to listen to a demo, let alone approve it for production, is a highly serendipitous affair. Even when that hurdle is crossed, people show up to the recording sessions late, the engineer gets sick, Linda Ronstadt has just covered the same song, the musical idea doesn't work, the digital delay malfunctions—and production continually has to adapt to these circumstances. Similarly, production always has unforeseen outcomes, both musical and otherwise. If that were not the case, the record business would be subject to less risk and a far lower rate of failure.

Yet regardless of the particularity or the unpredictability of any specific production process, production is not random; it occurs within limiting conditions that are themselves always in flux. All processes of musical production occur within the limiting conditions of musical reference, including both the musical vocabulary of different genres or large systems of musical meaning (such as tonality). As demonstrated in the case of rap, these don't function as static boundaries but are themselves subject to continual articulation. If, to take once again the extreme case, musical production results in a pop CD, the limiting conditions would also include what the record companies think they can sell, the flow of payments (which structure time), the technologically available forms of sound reproduction and industry standards of decision making. All of these—and it should be noted that they are functions not simply of the economy but also of science and the legal system—serve to ensure that what results from this process is a "product" that can be sold in existing conditions. But a jazz record or an independent rock production would occur within contingent articulations of the same conditions. For example, the flow of payments will structure time in any recording situation, but payment arrangements tend to vary both with the genre of music and with the involvement of lawyers in contract negotiations. Nor is the case of live musical performance substantially different, regardless of how different the product itself may be. True, the performance is sold in advance of its actual production (on spec, as it were), yet production still occurs within the limiting conditions of available technology, legal decisions and notions of salability, in addition to conditions of musical reference.

Contingency applies therefore not merely to the overall production process but to all of its components, and it necessitates continual selection. As an example, what the record companies think they can sell exists as a reservoir of possibilities, only some of which become actual constraints through structuring events such as decisions or communications. Proven stars, specific vocal techniques, horn arrangements, 2-bar vamps, drum machines, the Seattle sound, what's new but not too new—all of these represent a complexity that has to be managed in order for decisions to be made, the recording to be produced, and the system to function. As a limiting condition, what the record companies think they can sell can be articulated; it is in fact continually being articulated in endless variations on style and formula. However, selection is contingent and it is always provisional. The negated options that are a consequence of selection remain available; what the record companies think they can sell is never decided once and for all. The question is how those selections resonate as music or as information that becomes encoded in musical work.[6]

Luhmann presented the concept of resonance as a refinement of the input processing model that had informed his earlier work. It is defined as selective contact with the environment based on the system's "difference technique" (1989: 18). Rather than an actual transference of information from the environment or another social subsystem, data circulating within one subsystem can appear to another subsystem as information, given the specific distinctions that are made within that system. For example, the economy functions through ongoing payments, but only some of them, perhaps those made to politicians, will have resonance for the political system. In addition, events in one system can have a disproportionate effect in others, such as when what in economic terms is a small payment becomes a large political scandal. Resonance is a form of interpretation of information from one system to another. However, production is not merely interpretation but a form of actualization, and there is no mechanism in the existing model of open systems to account for it. This gap is arguably a by-product of conceptualizing every social process as communicative, and communication primarily in the medium of language. The question which remains to be addressed is how information from other subsystems becomes an aspect of music itself; that is, becomes material as sound. Translation describes how this occurs.

Translation is a system function, a means of actualizing information from other subsystems in musical production processes.[7] Whereas autopoietic selection presupposes meaning-constituting systems or complexes of meaning, translation presupposes complexes of actualization. Like meaning, these have temporal, material and social dimensions. They become established through repeated experience (in this case, the successful actualization of musical production), are responsive to the requirements of other subsystems and, in the case of music, are materialized as sound. As with meaning-based selection, contingency is also managed in translation, although it remains an inherent quality of all system operations. Translation establishes patterns of actualization between self-referential systems, which in turn account for the remarkable degree of similarity in otherwise contingent processes. Like meaning, translation functions as a premise but does not determine outcome.

Data from other subsystems that is recognized as information by the subsystem of music—that is, which resonates with music—may then be translated into music or translated with respect to music. The self-reference of meaning is maintained; money translated into music is not the same as money translated into science. Neither is translation a matter of one-to-one correspondence or equivalence. It is not analogous to translation from one language to another but from one meaning system to another. Money translated into science as, for instance, applied research does not yield the same thing as scientific truth translated into the economy in the form of rational capitalist economics, although they may be related. In the subsystem of music, resonant information from other subsystems can only be translated into music. The self-reference of meaning as a condition of the subsystem makes translation system specific. Translations are modes of actualization, not specific contents, and translation does not result in the signification or representation of other social subsystems in musical terms. Rather, it is a translation of this resonant information into the actual constitution of music and, as a result, of communication about music.

The example of the translation of money into music, or between the subsystems of the economy and music, has been an ongoing concern of cultural theory and one that is central to the question of aesthetic autonomy. It is also in this context that Luhmann suggests that differentiation is not completely successful for every social subsystem and raises the possibility of the economy colonizing the subsystem of art. How does the translation of money into music proceed, and what does it sound like? Money translated into music is first a currency of expectations. The decisions of record company executives and accountants about recording budgets and artists' salaries are always made with an eye toward sales; expectations about sales translate into expectations of musical production. Considerations of genre or of the musical ideas of particular artists are not incidental to the process, but they function less as aesthetic criteria than as expectations based on prior experience. More fundamentally, money buys and structures time. The sound of money in music is the sound of production rather than of any specific musical style, and the sound of musical production is a function primarily of how much time is spent and secondarily of the recording equipment used. The more time that is bought, the more contingency can be managed, in that musical mistakes can be corrected, songs can be mixed and remixed to achieve whatever is considered the desirable sound, and different combinations of songs and mix results can be circulated to get a sense of their commercial viability. Money also buys the use of new technology, which because it is new adds to the range of possibilities of sound production or reproduction. In addition, any new technology (recording or otherwise) is initially expensive and therefore represents money; its implication in music as a sound of money is immediate.[8] In the case of both time and technology, the translation of money into music increases the range of possible actualizations and requires a more complex selection process.

The translation of money into music isn't always successful; sometimes music sounds less like music than it does like the money invested in it. The likelihood of unsuccessful translation seems to grow with the amount of money involved, and this may be due to the fact that the increasing complexity that translation entails cannot always be successfully managed. However, there is no constant equation that can predict these outcomes and no critical mass point at which money will always overwhelm the ability of the subsystem of music to process it. The reason so much music sounds like money is that, given a certain level of capital investment, it is very often the lawyers and business people that are making the decisions. Yet this trajectory actually tends to reverse once a particular recording artist or star becomes so expensive that problems of material production are referred back to the subsystem of music, and the star, for resolution.[9] The distinction between music that sounds like music and music that sounds like money is not an either/or distinction but runs on a continuum of possible combinations of sounds.

Translation has variable musical effects and outcomes. Willie Nelson's records are very intimate and don't sound like money, but they undoubtedly cost a lot. The sound of money in jazz is not the same as the sound of money in pop music—right now it's a very polished, very straight sound, the sound of respectability. Even within a specific musical form like pop, the sound of money is not constant; indeed, like any good fashion, it changes every few years. In the 1980s the sound of money in pop music was very slick, drum machines were used extensively and the sound was built up from a very fat bottom, boosted way up for a dance mix. In order for vocals to carry over the bottom, certain high-end frequencies in the voice were accentuated—not the extreme highs, but somewhere toward the top of the range— and digital delay echo gave the voice a sheen to smooth out the edges. In the early 1990s the reaction to that sound in white music was grunge; in black music it was rap. Both represented a defiance of the money sound of the 1980s. Technically, vocals were recorded to sound cheap (i.e., recorded flat with no echo), and the overall production sound was very raw and unpolished. Ironically, the videos for these bands were unbelievably expensive, almost as though the money you were asked to overlook in its aural presentation was made immediately visible. With the shift to video as the medium of sales, the translation of money into music has developed a visual reflection.[10] The last few years have seen another shift toward a more polished sound in techno. Drum machines carry a house rhythm track as other music (original or not) is faded in and out. The resulting sound of money is a blend of the technological fetishism of the 1980s with a rap aesthetic.

If the money is not audible in music, it doesn't mean that it isn't there, just that it may not be the prominent or dominant sound. Even in pop songs, presumably made *as* money, other sounds may be more audible. There is a sound of time—as nostalgia, as history or as surprise. Music translates information from other subsystems as well in the process of production. There is a sound of religion, which has been fairly constant in Western classical music, although it has a contingent articulation in popular music such as gospel and Christian pop. The sound of power is grounded in classicist odes to empire, monarch or wealth; that of protest in rock 'n' roll and certain folk traditions. Music also has a sound of passion. Virtually all music made in our society is made with money and therefore translates money into music to some degree. Money translated into music is music as a commodity. Yet the simple reality of production in contemporary society does not therefore imply that all production that translates from the economy is linked to domination, much less that it sounds the same.

As a final note, resonance also structures the reception context for music. For example, the fact that rap stars have been in trouble with the law has become a feature of the reception context for that music; outlaw status is inseparable from the actual musical component of what is heard. With the concept of resonance, this can be explained as data from the legal system having resonated with, or been recognized as information by, the subsystem of music. Michael Jackson's highly publicized $50 million contract with Sony in 1990 similarly became an aspect of the reception context for his subsequent work, as did information about his alleged romantic involvement with, or sexual abuse of, young boys. The reception context for any musical work is always both musical and nonmusical; resonance is useful in conceptualizing how the nonmusical elements become aspects of musical reception. Resonance is also contingent, however, with respect to which data is recognized as information as well as to its actualization in communication about music. Not every contract price is an aspect of social communication; not every rumor sticks.

THE STRUCTURE OF THEORY /
AUTONOMY AND CRITIQUE

Rather than a deterministic model of musical production, such as the mass culture critique, translation is a highly mobile conceptualization from which outcome, musical or economic, cannot be predicted. As a consequence, musical work becomes central to analysis. Translation, like meaning, functions as a premise, but translation is also contingent and its effects cannot be analyzed without in this instance being heard. Reframing analysis through the work, both as the site of translation and as the limiting condition on autopoietic communication, has important ramifications. Foremost among them is that it makes critique possible.

Placing the musical work at the center of analysis does not imply a return to formal methods of aesthetic investigation, given that the musical work has been reconceptualized in sociological terms. It both organizes communications within the subsystem of music and is the site of translation from other subsystems. In other words, both social production processes and system reproduction processes are actualized through the musical work, which provides the basis from which these processes can be observed and their effects demonstrated. Following the logic, but not the aesthetic orientation, of Adorno's argument, only the musical work can be a site of critique.

Historically, critique has also been linked to the autonomy status of art, as the attack on autonomy and correlative retreat from critique in postmodern aesthetic theory demonstrates. According to Weber's account of the differentiation of value spheres, art was freed from its religious and courtly functions and could develop according to its own internal logic. Art as an autonomous social sphere was conceptualized as a domain set apart from society and this distance served an important critical function. Yet the conceptualization of autonomy vis-à-vis society has frequently been interpreted to mean that contact with other social domains could only be a form of contamination, or at the very least, signaled the loss of critical potential. Given contemporary conditions of musical production, in which translation is a constant feature, critique became increasingly difficult to imagine, much less pursue.

The model of open systems situates the autonomy of the subsystem of music *within* society. In so doing, it presents an important alternative to both static modernist conceptions of autonomy that have made critique problematic, and the postmodern rhetoric of dedifferentiation that renders it impossible. The formulation of autonomy within society also suggests a different way of conceptualizing Weber's narrative. At the same time that differentiation in the modern period established a distinctly musical terrain, it simultaneously opened up the production of music to other social subsystems, including the economy, science, the legal system, education and the emotional realm, in addition to its traditional moorings in church and state. Rather than representing a necessary decline, this simultaneous closure and openness has radically increased the possibilities of system actualizations. What this means in terms of critical strategies will be discussed in the following chapters.

Nevertheless, important questions remain as to how successful differentiation has been, or will continue to be, in the case of art and music. The outcome of translation with respect to system integrity is variable, and the possibility of the economy coloniz-ing the subsystem of music is more than a theoretical one. The crucial element here will be whether subsystem complexity in-creases or decreases in the process of recurrent distinction of the system from the environment. Increasing complexity of system actualizations would make colonization by another subsystem that much more difficult. If, however, recurrent distinction be-comes more streamlined, if it takes more static form, if fewer modes of actualization are realized, then the threat of other sub-systems would become more real. In a mode of differentiation where closure is a condition of openness, of the continual need to differentiate between system and environment, autonomy de-pends on outwitting other subsystems by staying one step ahead of the game. Increasing complexity of meaning within the sub-system would be the way to ensure that.

The basic thesis that has been presented here, that music is an autopoietic social subsystem that is both open with respect to its environment and closed with respect to meaning, brings together in the same formulation the notions of the social nature of music and its autonomy. Rather than self-reference and social func-tion being mutually exclusive, they appear in systems theory as mutually implied, or as reciprocal aspects of the system/ environment distinction. Given a self-reflective theory of art, "it is understandable that any social function of art is frequently disputed and its autonomy equated with absence of function." Luhmann continues, "You can sign the death sentence in this way. Or you can revise the foundations of theory" (1990: 213).

NOTES

1. This formulation is derived from Niklas Luhmann's (1990) theory of autopoietic (self-reproducing) social systems.

2. Mead's idea of passage from one system to another links the concept of sociality to temporality. The idea that such passage effects a change in both systems prefigures a dynamic rather than a static concept of system and environment.

3. In his early work, Luhmann relied on an information-processing model that he later came to criticize as inadequate to describe social processes. However, autopoeisis, the replacement model, also requires some elaboration. What I propose here is not collapsing early and late Luhmann but rather a critical adaptation of autopoeisis, which depends on new additions to the model.

4. According to Ann Palkovich (personal communications), a time-sensitive concept of authenticity would breathe new life into a concept which has become a dead-end in anthropological research and debate.

5. Niklas Luhmann (1982: 265). "We may presume here that the different functional domains have unequal chances for development. For example, it is by no means assured in a complex, highly differentiated society (in which science and economic life obviously flourish) that satisfactory combinations of function, performance, and self-reflection can be found for religion or for art. To this extent, the evolution of society has emphatically 'selective' consequences for what remains possible in its later stages." This argument is reproduced in *Essays on Self-Reference* (1990: 213).

6. To the extent that they produce new musical work and therefore more communication about music, musical production processes have an autopoietic function. However, they cannot be accounted for solely as aspects of autopoietic reproduction, as Luhmann seems to suggest in his later work. According to Luhmann, the self-reference of meaning ensures that musical works both refer to other musical works and simultaneously reproduce the system. Yet this understanding of musical production is only adequate to describe forms of production that have minimal reference to other social subsystems, in which autopoiesis is responsible for the production of all system components. Whether intentional or not, Luhmann's analysis of production as self-reproduction only pertains to a high art notion of music. The very concept of "high art" is based on the self-reference of art and therefore is much more compatible with the structure of the theory. The problem is that, whether or not we still have "high art," its traditional modes of production no longer substantially exist.

7. The conceptualization is based on, and intended to describe, the

social system of art. I leave it to other scholars to ascertain whether or not it is adequate to explain the functioning of other social systems.

8. The fact that technology is expensive when new and then gets cheaper is resonant information from the subsystem of science. The development of new and expensive drum machines in the 1980s is an interesting example of the ongoing translation between the economy, science and music. This new technology allowed for both a wider range and a more precise control of frequencies as well as control over attack and decay, which produced a sharper, cleaner sound. Whether the technology was developed to conform to the industry truism that white audiences go for a cleaner sound (whereas black audiences go for bass-heavy sounds) or was developed for the sake of technological advance itself would be difficult to know with certainty, but it is highly suggestive.

9. Of course, one could pick up Adorno's ([1938] 1982) argument that the star is him- or herself a product of translations from the economy, or a commodity fetish.

10. In a sense, this supports Adorno's ([1938] 1982) arguments about commodity fetishism—the industry sells music and people buy it, not as music but as the money it represents.

4

CRITIQUE

The problem of critique that is the legacy of the Frankfurt School is that of critique from within. Where is the space for alternatives in a totalizing model of society, where domination is reproduced in every instance of thought? Attempts to give this "space" a functional interpretation have proven inadequate, both in theory and in actual social practice. It cannot inhere in a particular social domain (in which freedom and constraint are simultaneously present), in a particular social group (which is internally complex), in a particular mode of thought (in which there are multiple tendencies) or in a specific aesthetic form that can be designated as "autonomous." Nevertheless, and in spite of the theoretical difficulty, the critique of ideology and of social institutions has been ongoing, even among postmodern theorists for whom critique has no epistemological status. Theory has to recognize and account for the persistence of critique as actual social practice and to re-create the space for alternatives within its own domain.

Adorno captures critique as an ideal, but other conceptual tools are needed to overcome the reification of dialectics and to realize critical theory. I have appropriated some of these tools from Luhmann, although the appropriation of elements of Luhmann's work for critical theory is certainly one that he didn't intend. Yet I am not proposing that systems theory can serve as a replacement paradigm for critical theory, rather that a selective utilization of some these ideas can serve in the construction of new theory. Foremost among them are the notions of contingency as a form of differentiation, complexity as a description of social systems and temporality as a constitutive dimension of all social phenomena.

Temporality is also constitutive of critique. Temporality is necessary for critique because critique is both in the present and reaches beyond the present to what is potential, to what might have been or to a possible utopia. It is the criticism of what actually exists against those possibilities, past or future. In critique these temporal possibilities are juxtaposed and time is presented within time. Any critical theory must have some way of looking at the relations between differentiated components, such as action spheres, forms of ideology or social actors. . . . In the framework developed here, the space for alternatives exists as differentiated temporality.

TEMPORAL STRUCTURE OF CRITIQUE

In the tradition of marxist scholarship that includes the Frankfurt School, critique was structured as a confrontation between what is and what could be, or between the actual and the potential. In the early Marx of "On the Jewish Question" ([1843] 1975b) critique is a confrontation between reality as the actual present, the real historical conditions of modern society and norms that are transhistorical or transcendent. In the "Economic and Philosophical Manuscripts" ([1844] 1975) the reality of alienation is posed against a vision of utopia; present actuality is made to confront a possible future. One of the strengths of marxist analysis and critique has been its emphasis on the historicity of the present, on the idea that what is is not eternal but rather a product of human labor and imagination and therefore subject to change. Of the Frankfurt theorists, Herbert Marcuse was perhaps most eloquent on the subject of history and its relation to critique. In his early essay "The Struggle Against Liberalism in the Totalitarian View of the State" ([1968] 1988), Marcuse criticized naturalism and universalism as denials of human history and exposed their role in the self-justification of totalitarianism. The thesis of *One-Dimensional Man* (1964) is also about history, about the elimination of the dialectical tension between what is and what has been and therefore what could be. One-dimensional society generates an operational rationality and a functionalized language that are anti-historical and that eliminate the possibility of critique. For example, what passes for democracy in the one-dimensional society *is* democracy; all of its historical possibilities and contradictions are reduced to the forms in which it currently operates. In these conditions, history serves an important critical function, and its suppression is an important political matter.

[T]he tension between the "is" and the "ought," between essence and appearance, potentiality and actuality ... permeates the two-dimensional universe of discourse which is the universe of critical abstract thought. The two dimensions are antagonistic to each other; the reality partakes of both of them, and the dialectical concepts develop the real contradictions. In its own development, dialectical thought came to comprehend the historical character of the contradictions and the process of their mediation as historical process. Thus the "other" dimension of thought appeared to be *historical* dimension—the potentiality as historical possibility, its realization as historical event. (97)

Critical thought is a form of historical consciousness, for remembrance is "a mode of mediation which breaks, for short moments, the omnipresent power of the given facts" (98).

Adorno's aesthetic critique reproduces the dialectical structure of actual and potential, is and ought. However, where history draws its potential from the past, the potential of art is oriented toward the future. According to Adorno, the truth of art was the depiction of the truth about society, a truth it was nevertheless able to transcend. Adorno conceptualized the ability of art as critique to transcend social reality as an ability to be outside domination, commodification or the reification of Enlightenment rationality. Standpoint, conceptualized in spatial terms such as these, became extremely problematic given the totalizing context of modernity. However, standpoint is a matter of time as well, and this is implicit in Adorno's formulation. Transcendence was the hope of redemption, the potential for emancipation, which in the conditions of modern society was always oriented toward the future. Both the critique of art and art as critique are situated in and represent the present at the same time that they go beyond the present. The potential in art is utopian, the potential to imagine a world that does not yet exist. In critique, this utopian potential is counterposed to the present actuality of art itself.

Yet art as critique and, ultimately, critical theory were antinomic. Adorno observed that in the conditions of total administration, critical art was severed from its social base, and critical theory ran the risk of becoming a form of resistance in a vacuum. Adorno believed that this had to do with the level of difficulty of critical art or the hostility of the ignorant who identified with fetishized commodities ([1938] 1982). However, there is another, less Freudian, explanation. No vision of the future, no idea of the potential, can reenter a static world. One of the defining aspects of modernity for Adorno was that history itself was at a standstill, the totally administered world was by definition static. If art is the ability to picture a world that does not yet exist, if critique draws on a potential that is not currently being actualized in social conditions, then they represent a possible future, one that has no place in a world in which time stands still.

What I want to underscore and to make explicit here is the implicit concern with time in the structure of critique within this intellectual tradition. The problem as I see it is that time was understood in purely historical terms, and these historical categories lent themselves to reification. The recognized historicity of the present, which is a description of its contingency, was subordinated to the overdetermined character of marxist theory, to a teleology that constructs the present as a fixed relation to past and future. The distinction between the period of liberal capitalism and that of monopoly capitalism, for instance, was virtually absolute—that the past as such continued to be present in the present was not recognized. Similarly, the future was conceptualized only as a radical change from the present, rather than holding the potential for preservation or conservation as well.[1] This understanding of time was an aspect of most narratives of modernity that tended to conceal the temporal complexity of a world that was both contiguous with and radically changed from the past, in which progress coexisted with tradition and in which prediction from given conditions worked only some of the time. However, the reification of historical categories also accounts for the fact that the judgments made about art in the name of history take on a character of necessity that is no longer credible.

Rather than a description of social conditions as static and totalizing or grounded in historical categories that tend to reification, social systems are dynamic and have the potential to be temporally complex. This is particularly true in music and other subsystems of art, where time itself is often suspended and temporal complexity can be sustained; where the imperative of making sense and getting on to the next event may be mediated by remembrance, contemplation, or anticipation, all extensions of time. In this context, the distinction between the actual and the potential is not the difference between the historical conditions of modernity and either a historical past or a utopian future. Rather, the potential appears within the actual as the presentation of time within time.

In the critique of music, what is actual is the present, the actual constitution of music in performance and reception. The potential is both past and future, as existing criteria or standards and as the space opened up by surprise. Music's potential to be great music, by any standards and in any style or tradition, always has both a past and a future referent. It can only be as good or better than something known, and in a way that cannot be anticipated. The past enters the present as forms of organizing material that ensure their intelligibility, as social expectations of how music makes sense. In addition to serving as a set of established criteria for making music, prior judgments about music serve as standards to be met or superseded. The future in music is not merely innovation, or what is new, or a vision of utopia; it is also a process stimulated by surprise. Surprise generates the present as a distinction from past and future; without it there are no events, only the arrival of what is expected. However, surprise also moves into the future in that its normalization is an extended process; it requires more time. A space for the future is implicated within music as the temporal trajectory or time it will take to normalize surprising information or to readjust to shifting premises. For surprise is not only innovation, a category associated with modern art, but also the denial of premises associated with forms of entertainment like carnival and the circus.

Critique situated in the present, rather than in the "historical moment" or the historical conditions of modernity, is a communicative event that generates more communication. It is an event situated within a dynamic social subsystem, and it participates in its autopoiesis. More than simply a moment in an endless chain of similarly structured moments, however, critique is situated in the present but also reaches beyond the present. Critique presents the potential within the actual as the past and future in the present, as standards and surprise within the actuality of musical performance and reception. Critique is not the process of resolving these temporal distinctions or reducing them to a single historical judgment. It has the character of passage; its temporal structure requires being in two places at once, a present becoming past and a future emerging as present.

If critique is situated in the present, the judgments of critique are not historical but eventful, not final but contingent. This does not mean that they lack conviction or commitment or that they do not engage standards or criteria that can be articulated. What it does suggest is that these judgments are open to being confirmed, restated, rejected or superseded because they occur, they emerge and disappear, in time. Unlike art, critique is always in time rather than experienced as time out of time. Critique is therefore imminently social—both in Luhmann's terms as communication and in George Herbert Mead's as temporal, as an event that has the character of being in more than one time at a time and changing the character of both.

Adorno wrote, "Above all, the meaning of a work of art is also the summoning to appearance of an essence that is otherwise hidden in empirical reality" ([1970] 1984: 154). I would suggest instead that critique brings the potential forward as presence, not as essence. It opens out and can sustain the space for past and future as temporal possibilities within the present, rather than as utopian images that cannot reenter a static world.

FORM AND CONTEXT

Critique is a process of making distinctions. However, distinction is only meaningful within a given context, just as context is crucial to the way distinction functions. In order to formulate critique, both the form and the context of distinction must be taken into account. In Chapter 2, contingency was discussed as the form of distinction; in what follows, complexity will serve as a description of context. If structure or context itself is dynamic, distinction can escape the reification that is a consequence of static or closed systems.

Complexity is a description of structure as a dynamic whole comprised of shifting parts with multiple interrelations. It provides the context for critique as both the structure of theory and that of social systems. That complexity is an advance over dialectics in theorizing social organization is borne out in a great deal of contemporary theory and analysis; any work that discusses multiple as opposed to binary relations, or that conceptualizes social organization as a network of relations that are continually yet contingently exercised, already points in that direction. For instance, Foucault's conception of power as "the multiplicity of force relations immanent in the sphere in which they operate and which constitute their own organization" (1978:

92) illustrates complexity as both multiple relations and self-organization. Using complexity as a model also avoids the pitfall of conceptualizing structure as random and fragmented.

A dialectical model of critique, based on the subject/object dualism, is not adequate because it cannot account for the multiplicity of possible relations. Luhmann only addresses the question of critique in the most tangential way as something anomalous, an alternative structure or possible utopia "brought to light by uncovering some latent aspect of the existing order, or retrieved from the existing decision-making process by incongruent questions" (1990: 34). Indeed, the tendency of systems is to normalize information in autopoietic communication. Given that there is no model of critique within this framework,[2] I will proceed first by looking at the relation between the form and the context of critique in Adorno's work. Second, I will consider how distinction functions in a different context—that of complex social systems—and how, or whether, that can be brought in line with the temporal requirements of critique.

Distinctions constitute space as relative positions and articulate time as implied events; distinctions not only make boundaries but also define relationships. In other words, distinctions both occur in a context and recursively structure the context. For Adorno, the negative dialectic as a form created a distance, a space in which critique could arise. The "uneasy tension" between art and society was not an empty space but a contested one. Art had the potential to be critique because it was autonomous from society in a dialectical sense—distant but related, identical and nonidentical:

For no authentic work of art and no true philosophy, according to their very meaning, has ever exhausted itself in itself alone, in its being-in-itself. They have always stood *in relation* to the actual life-process of society from which they *distinguished* themselves. (1981 [1967]: 23; emphasis added)

The form of the negative dialectic also established transcendent and immanent positions with respect to the work. Finally, the distinction of autonomy as social differentiation became internalized or aestheticized as a quality inhering in actual works of art. In Adorno's work, the form of social differentiation became the content of critique.

Yet the dialectical character of autonomy as the form of social differentiation and of critique could not be sustained in the totalizing context of social administration and Enlightenment rationality. At the same time that this context provided the stimulus for critique, it contributed to its reification and eventual antinomy. Within this context, distinctions were operationalized as opposition to the overarching social order. The function of distinction was to open up spaces of negativity in which the nonidentical could exist. But the context, described by Adorno not only as total but also as static and closed, could not accomodate the existence of difference that nevertheless stands in relation to society. The dynamic aspect of dialectics was reduced to a choice either to conform or to escape. If the autonomy of art was not exercised, the distinction between art and society would collapse. Art would become, as in the case of mass culture, the reproduction of ideology. However, when the autonomy of art was exercised, as in the case of great art such as Schoenberg's music, it became severed from its social base. In this case, identity and nonidentity come to function not as a dynamic and dialectical pair but as a contradiction, an opposition that necessitates taking sides.[3]

Adorno came to criticize the binary structure of dialectics as reductive, observing that we encounter not only the thing and its other but a multiplicity of things in dynamic relations to one another.[4] This notion, expressed in *Negative Dialectics*, is an early articulation of complexity.[5] According to Luhmann, social systems are internally complex in that it is not possible to interrelate every element with every other element in the system. Furthermore, there is no one-to-one correspondence between self-reference and external reference; it is not possible to relate every element of the system with its environment (1990: 81). In either instance, the number of possible relations is simply too large.

Complexity therefore enforces selection, which simultaneously reduces complexity vis-à-vis the environment and allows for an increase of complexity among the elements of the system.

An analysis of music illuminates the development of self-referential subsystems based on selection from the environment. Of all of the available sounds, only certain ones generated by certain instruments (e.g., not toilets flushing or cows mooing) are considered musical. Those selections reduce the number of possible elements of the system. Yet at the same time they also create the conditions in which highly specific and highly complex forms of musical organization can be established that link these elements together. The increasing complexity of systems of notation and forms of composition in Europe, for instance, arose with the modern period and the identification of a functionally distinct and autonomous domain of music. The rationalization of instrument making in accordance with the requirements of composition and performance, increasing professionalization and the concomitant exclusion of amateurs and homemade instruments can all be understood as consequences of a growing selectivity.[6] In the contemporary period, the self-reference of music is more stable and therefore can accommodate more risk. This has resulted less in an increase of complexity with respect to compositional forms than in terms of the number of elements, and therefore relations between elements, available within the system. More sounds are considered musical, including feedback, industrial sounds, turntables scratching, screaming, silence and environmental sounds. The ability to manage risk also speaks to the widespread acceptance of improvisation.

The social subsystem of music is also internally complex in that it is impossible to link every communication to every other communication, or every event to other events. Again, the number of possible combinations is too large. Our descriptions of the subsystem will therefore always be selective. For example, any description of the music business as a fully rationalized system, or as one based on the intuitions of A&R (artists and repertoire) executives, is a result of contingent selections. The relations between events that result in a signed recording contract are not overdetermined. Selections are not, however, by definition counterfactual, nor does selection imply that every description of the music business is more or less a fiction. Granted, observation takes place within the system, and that places certain limitations on what one can observe. We cannot see totality; there will always be blind spots. But more complex descriptions—those that account for a greater number of dynamic relations between elements—yield a better picture.

With regard to critique, the question is how, in the context of complex social systems, distinctions are operationalized. How does distinction function? Whereas for Adorno distinction serves negativity or opposition with respect to the total social system, for Luhmann distinction is a means of managing complexity and is implicated in system reproduction. Luhmann draws his conceptual framework of distinction and form from G. Spencer Brown's *Laws of Form*, the first sentence of which reads as follows: "We take as given the idea of distinction and the idea of indication, and that we cannot make an indication without drawing a distinction" (1972: 1). Distinction serves not critique but *indication*—literally, pointing to something. Dynamic social systems are always generating communications and processing information. Given the multiple possible relations of any new communication to any other element of the system, social systems must have a mechanism for coping with the constant influx of information. Selection, based on meaning, manages complexity in system operations. Selection occurs through making distinctions—the distinction between the potential of possible meanings and that which is being actualized—and routinely proceeds through normalization. That is, "the unknown is assimilated to the known, the new to the old, the surprising to the familiar" (Luhmann, 1990: 33). Distinction in Luhmann's model is not, as it was for Adorno, setting up a tension between oppositional concepts but rather deciding what things are, and most often making selections in accordance with what already is. As a consequence, although systems theory is based on distinction and articulates social systems as complex, the impulse to critique is neutralized.

TEMPORALITY

If distinction is to function as critique, it must open up time or create a tension between temporal possibilities. It must produce temporal complexity. In the instance described above, complexity is reduced in the constitution of present experience. Indication is the present; it is a matter of deciding what things are so that systems can manage communicative surprises and get on to the next event. From the point of view of temporality, autopoiesis is solely concerned with the constitution of the present. This is a reductive picture, however, one that stands to be revised in light of other conceptions of temporality in sociology and the specific temporality of music.[7] Music serves as a window to temporality in that its complexity is also and always temporal.

For Luhmann, time is not just the parameter within which social life takes place, nor can time be "treated merely as a category underlying our knowledge of social life." On the contrary, "temporality . . . becomes a constitutive dimension of its [sociology's] subject matter" (1982: 290). Like Mead ([1932] 1959), Luhmann situates sociality in the present, a present constituted by events. He also draws specifically on Husserl's phenomenology in conceptualizing past and future as horizons that are both integrated in and constitutive of the present. Rather than seeing time as passing or as segmented and measured, Luhmann shares with a philosophical tradition that reaches from Augustine to Bergson to Heidegger a concern with temporality as constitutive time. Translated into systems theory, eventfulness and temporality constitute difference, insofar as the present is the difference between past and future.

Systems based on events need a more complex pattern of time. For them, time cannot be given as irreversibility only. Events are happenings that make a difference between a "before" and a "thereafter."

Events can be identified and observed, anticipated and remembered only as such a difference. Their identity is difference. Their presence is a copresence of the before and the thereafter. They have, therefore to present time within time. (1990: 10)

Nevertheless, there is a tension in Luhmann's model of auto-poiesis between this idea of a temporally complex present, one in which time is presented within time, and the function of se-lection based on meaning to reduce complexity. The moment of constituting experience is always temporally complex, but ex-perience itself, which is only possible in the present, is consti-tuted through the reduction of this complexity.[8] Conventional musicological descriptions of listening to music provide an ex-ample of how this process works. According to musicologist Leonard Meyer (1956), musical meaning takes the form of co-herence; that is, making sense out of music through grasping patterns, fitting new information into these patterns, or altering the patterns to accommodate new information. As one listens, selections are made that conform to established or accepted meaning, and new information is routinely normalized. "Reflec-tion is brought into play only when a pattern of habitual behav-ior is disturbed" (39). From the vantage point of systems theory, selection is always provisional in that it stands to be revised in light of new information. From the perspective of phenomenol-ogy, listening to music is a constant revision of expectations, which include protention and retention in listening, socially con-structed expectations of genre and the fact that resolution is often prefigured in compositional form. As Luhmann (1990: 45) says, the sociality of expectations is not that of actual behavior but of expectation itself. In other words, what we expect musically are not specific elements of composition but patterns of actualiza-tion, and we attempt to fit what we hear into those patterns. Through selection, we accomplish the ongoing constitution of the present at the same time that the complexity of possible relations between musical elements is reduced.

Luhmann suggests that complexity is reduced in each moment

of constitution, making ongoing communication possible, but it is preserved in the world as the source of possibilities.

> Complexity cannot simply be "erased," as computer jargon puts it . . . but is, so to speak, only placed in brackets, reduced from moment to moment in continually different ways, and always remains preserved as the most generally constituted selection domain, as the "source" of constantly new and constantly different additional choices—as the world. (1990: 27)

The two sides of this distinction are the reduction and preservation of complexity. But the complexity preserved here is simply a "reservoir" of possible relations. It is a medium that does not exhibit a temporality of its own, in which there is no meaningful conception of past, present or future. Its structure is, as Mead once remarked of Newtonian physics ([1932] 1959: 40), irrelevant to time, given that the possibilities of which it consists are timeless. "To the extent that time leaves the future open and all possibilities possible, it is the ongoing, immediate present of actual lived experience that becomes problematic" (Luhmann, 1990: 41). The past has some importance as the structure of systems, as capital, in the sense of an accumulation of money or knowledge or power. However, like memory and writing, history cannot preserve the events themselves, only their ability to generate structure. Therefore, temporal complexity, as the presentation of time within time, cannot be sustained. Caught between a relentless present and an atemporal world, it simultaneously comes to be and is eradicated in the moment of constituting experience. What is actual is merely selection from a potential that remains unchanged.

George Herbert Mead's work suggests other ways of understanding events and the temporal structure of the present that can inform, and is in fact closely related to, systems theory. According to Mead,

> A present . . . is not a piece cut out anywhere from the temporal dimension of uniformly passing reality. Its chief reference is to the emergent

event, that is, to the occurrence of something which is more than the processes that have led up to it and which by its change, continuance or disappearance, adds to later passages a content they would not otherwise have possessed. ([1932] 1959: 23)

In Mead's conception of social reality as ceaseless emergence, it is events in relation to other events that structure time and mark out a past and a future; indeed, "time only exists in these distinctions" (20). Yet what occurs in this eventful present is not the constitution of experience through a reduction of complexity but what Mead refers to as "passage." Out of each event, each moment of emergence, a process of mutual readjustment arises as new phenomena interact with the old. The social character of emergence inheres in the fact that "the novel event is in both the old order and the new one which its advent heralds" (49). In passage, the old and the new are mutually implicated in emergent relations that reflect back on the older world, even as older relations are reflected in the new system. As Barbara Adam observes:

Sociality then is located in that process of adjustment and not in its result, in being part of the old and the new at the same time. Sociality could therefore be described as the dynamic meeting, the interpenetration of continuity and change, of conservation and revolution. (1990: 40)

Sociality is, according to Mead, "the capacity of being several things at once" (49), which in this context implies being in a number of different worlds, orders or systems at once (these terms are used interchangeably) or being in several temporalities at once. Aside from the broad implication that sociality is temporal, what is important here is that events give rise to passage, which generates and sustains, rather than reduces and preserves, temporal complexity. Each event sets in motion multiple temporal relations to other events and, in passage, presents time within time.

Although it might be difficult to establish the general validity of this principle, it does produce a truer description of the temporal structure of listening to music. Listening is not merely the constitution of present experience through the revision of expectation but also the sociality of being in more than one temporal perspective at the same time. Sometimes music is simply coherence or the fulfillment of expectations. If there are no surprises, we simply go along with music as it goes along. But surprising information—an abrupt harmonic shift or the entrance of an instrument not usually associated with the type of music we're listening to—can arrest our attention and make it necessary to cope with this anomalous information at the same time that we continue to listen in "the present." Surprising information is simultaneously in the new and the old order, and it reconfigures our sense of both what has occurred before and what is to come. We may need to rethink what we have already heard to make it congruent with this new information. It may throw into doubt our sense of how the song or composition is going to resolve. It may be only a momentary diversion from prior experience and expectations, in which the surprising information is easily normalized. Normalization can also take time, confusion can last and a new musical order may or may not emerge as a coherent one.

If listening is not perfect coherence, neither is it pure attention. Surprising information can also take the form of a phrase that stimulates a memory of some other song or moment, a random sound coming from the next apartment, or a new thought that pops up in the moment of listening. What are normally thought of as "associations" always have the character of temporal differentiation. They emerge in the present but are not specific to the present as elements being actualized in constituting experience. More than simply making sense, indicating or fitting music into coherent patterns, the experience of listening is also in this sense a passage, occupying more than one time at a time.

What this suggests is that events structure time, but not all events structure time the same way. Every event marks out a present as a distinction between past and future, but each present emerges in contingent temporal relations to both the old and the new. For example, any new musical genre, song, or set of production criteria always appears as a relation to older ones (radically different, contiguous, derivative, a pastiche) and constructs the past anew as it opens up a space into the future. Rap is seen as the culmination of the West African griot tradition at the same time that it introduces production techniques that over time become normalized as industry standards. With its introduction, what was considered cutting edge may now seem dated or at least thrown into a kind of temporal limbo. However, not every new event produces radical change; normalization can be simultaneous with the event or it can take time; some events are of short duration while others have a longer temporal reach. A new pop song that reproduces the current industry formula is easily grasped and just as easily discarded; as an event, its becoming and disappearing can be virtually simultaneous. (Hence the industry maxim that if the song doesn't sell in the first six weeks, it never will.) On the other hand, many jazz records become "classics" and sell over long periods of time because their emergence in the present is strongly connected with the past as a specific musical and social history. Of course, temporal claims both to newness, what has never been heard before, and to a legacy of past greatness are of tremendous significance in most art worlds as the basis on which art is valued.

To summarize, in music as in other social systems, distinction functions to reduce complexity in the constitution of present experience. Events, or surprising information, have to be managed immediately in order to be intelligible. This is accomplished through selection based on meaning. For Luhmann, selection proceeds through negation, a binary yes or no, this meaning and not that one. It is the distinction between the actualized meaning and those that remain potential. However, events not only construct the present but also simultaneously reconfigure all other temporal referents. Therefore, while the distinction of the present as a present reduces complexity in the normalization of surprising events or new information, it also generates complexity with respect to time. This temporal complexity is particularly sustainable in art and music and explains why they are important sites of critique.

The understanding of art as a sphere of contemplation, reflection or critique is based on its complexity, on multiple possible relations between elements, and between the work and the world. Art has also been described as liminality, as a realm of the senses or of the irrational. Given the social conditions of art in modern society, including its rationalization and commercialization, these descriptions do not fully apply. However, the differences they articulated between art and other forms of social practice can be reframed with respect to complexity and time. Rather than having to decide what things are in art, what they mean, and how they function, art is a domain in which complexity can be sustained. Multiple relations between elements, or between the work and the world, may resolve or be structured in aesthetic form. But art is valued, among other things, precisely as a relief from indication in the present, for its "faculty of arresting our attention and moving us" (Arendt, [1954] 1977a: 204). Durkheim described this sense of suspension in art and ritual as the experience of time out of time. Art takes place in an eventful present, but it has the potential to sustain the present, or disrupt the present, opening out the possibilities of time. The complexity of art or music is therefore not only a matter of relations between elements but also of temporality, which makes it compatible with the temporal structure of critique.

Finally, surprise is the catalyst for temporal complexity in that it creates discontinuity within the continuity of time and presents the need to reconfigure existing temporal relations. Only surprise makes us aware of time. Surprise is a form of difference; it causes the present to emerge as a distinction between past and future. Yet what occurs in the present is not simply indication through selection but a process—passage—that can be, and in music often is, sustained. The present cannot be conceptualized as a sequence of events passing through time or as an endless "now" moving into the future. Like music, the present as emergence and passage has tempo, and negotiates stability and instability, fixity and flux, continuity and disjuncture. Surprise is both the articulation of temporal difference and the possibility of its duration, not as a single moment extended over time but as ongoing process. Finally, because it opens up time and creates a tension between temporal possibilities, surprise can function as a distinction of critique. It generates temporal differentiation as the space in which alternatives can arise.

THE SPACE FOR ALTERNATIVES

The problem Horkheimer and Adorno confronted but failed to resolve in *Dialectic of Enlightenment* was the problem of critique from within. Given the totalizing character of Enlightenment reason, any mediation, any forms of self-reflection were already compromised in that they utilized the categories of Enlightenment thought. In earlier versions of marxist theory, spaces outside domination existed for alternatives such as working-class consciousness and, later, autonomous subjectivity. By the 1930s however, with the consolidation of state-centered forms of capitalism and authoritarianism, and the mobilization of workers in support of these tendencies, faith in these alternatives evaporated. The conception of modernity as a totalizing form of domination (both as socioeconomic structure and as the production of consciousness) led the critical theorists to the paradox of being situated in, but nevertheless looking for a standpoint outside of, the social system.[9]

In the model of society described by systems theory, any position in space, any standpoint, will be within a differentiated social domain; there is no point "outside." Horkheimer and Adorno were in fact right; relativity theory confirms that it is not possible to be outside an observing system. Yet the consequent relation between social practice and social structure or between micropractices and domination is neither as self-evident nor as dire as they presumed, or as has been presumed in the work of theorists like Foucault and Louis Althusser. Horkheimer and Adorno's conception that every instance of rational thought is a reproduction of Enlightenment domination is taken over in Althusser's (1971) pervasive (and nondialectical) concept of ideology. If all thought and all forms of reflection reproduce the ideology of the state, then there is no social practice and no social institution that can claim any autonomy from the state apparatus. Structure is static, and social practice is merely reproductive. For Foucault, structure as a self-organizing network is dynamic, but in a very particular sense. Power, according to Foucault ([1977] 1995), is not only productive but also "self-amplifying." The micropractices by which it is produced become more pervasive and find loci outside of their original institutional parameters. For instance, surveillance is not just an institutional practice of the prison system; the panopticon is also internalized by the inmates, who begin to police themselves. Institutional practices become consolidated as broad forms of social control.[10] The discourse of sexuality and the micropractices by which it is produced becomes the administration of bodies, populations and so forth (1978).

In these analyses, social practice and social structure are fully implicated in one another. Indeed, it cannot be otherwise, given the spatial notions of structure on which they are based. Structure as a relation of part to whole plays out in Althusser, as in Horkheimer and Adorno, reproductively: the parts reproduce the whole. For Foucault, structure is the sum of its parts. The dynamic or self-amplifying aspect of structure is merely the consequence of multiplication. Structure based on spatial relations of part to whole can only be reproductive or additive, not innovative, and therefore tends toward the reproduction of sameness rather than of difference. As a result, the possibility of alternatives implicit in the notion of autonomy, that is, alternatives based on differentiation, cannot be actualized. This obtains even in Foucault's work, where contingency is present with respect to both micropractices and instances of power.

The same is true of structure and agency models in sociology, including recursive ones like those of Anthony Giddens (1984) and Bourdieu. Both structuration and habitus conceptualize social structure as habit; structure has a kind of virtual existence through rules and resources, and the primary process of structuration is repetition. In systems theory, on the other hand, structure is emergent. According to Luhmann, structures are structures not of habit but of expectations. Where habit predetermines the reproduction of action, expectation connects events together across temporal distance, or as they move into the future. Social systems "develop structures capable of connecting action-events together. In this function (and not in a more or less lengthy, unchanging permanence) structures find their primary relationship to time, because connection can be accomplished only in time" ([1984] 1995: 288). A system itself is not a structure but a meaning system for communications. Complex systems form structures, but these structures are not productive in the sense that they produce particular kinds of actions or communications. They are not the actual relations between elements but the capacity of connecting events together, or "how permissible relations are constrained within the system" (283).

Unlike spatial notions of structure, which reproduce sameness, temporal notions of structure reproduce difference as the difference from one event to the next. In addition, the ongoing production of social systems is operationalized through differentiation. It is patterned on the reproduction of the system/ environment distinction within the system itself, as the distinction between self-reference and external reference. Like the presentation of time within time, or of autonomy within society, distinction is reinscribed in the space of the distinction. Yet reinscription does not eliminate the distance from the object necessary for critique, nor is it merely a form of infinite regress. In other words, distinction does not collapse into the reproduction of sameness, obviating the possibility of critique from within as it would in a spatial model of structure. Because structure is emergent, reinscription can never be perfect recurrence, there is always a temporal difference. No distinction is ever an exact reproduction of any other because it is always a new event and in the meantime the context has changed. This is not to suggest that there are no patterns of expectations, that emergence is random or that expectations do not function as constraints. Nor does it ignore the possibility that what is new or surprising may be so quickly normalized as to be virtually unrecognizable as new. Nevertheless, structure as the structure of expectations keeps available a range of possibilities, just as all events "contain an aspect of surprise, are new combinations of determinacy and indeterminacy" (291). As a consequence, it opens up rather than forecloses the possibilities of action and communication.[11]

Autonomy from within, and therefore the possibility of critique from within, are real and sustainable possibilities in a temporalized model of structure. Distinction occurs within the space of the distinction, there is no standpoint "outside." Rather than collapsing into sameness or blindly reproducing structure, however, temporality ensures that distinction can be distinct, that every new event is new. The possibility of alternatives is thus always present and can be actualized through contingent selections that constitute both social structure and social practice. Differentiated temporality creates the "space" or "distance" in which alternatives can arise. The more that temporal differentiation can be sustained, the greater the space for alternatives. Whether or not they will arise, whether or not critique is actualized or remains merely potential, is always contingent.

CONCLUSION

The aim of this chapter has been to re-create the space for critique and for alternatives within theory. I do not claim to have made possible in the world something that was not possible before; on the contrary, the possibility of alternatives and the potential for critique are always and already present, even in repressive circumstances. My argument has been that the structure of theory, in particular the spatial models used in sociology, has privileged the analysis of social constraints, social reproduction and social structure at the expense of social processes and their embeddedness in time. As a result, they do not account for difference as alternatives to what already exists, and social practices based on differentiation, such as critique, cannot be meaningfully situated in these models. This applies even in instances where critique is the explicit intent.

This analysis complements the work of other scholars in critical theory attempting to integrate critique into more fluid models of social organization and more fragmented models of thought. For example, both Craig Calhoun (1995) and Andreas Huyssen (1986) have criticized Habermas's (1981) holistic conception of modernity as an emancipatory project linked to the rationalist Enlightenment. Both argue that it comprises more than one tendency, and therefore different possibilities for the production of knowledge, and of critique, become possible. The argument is that the space for alternatives exists within modernity because it is complex. But recognizing complexity as different tendencies within one structure—that is, as spatial complexity—solves only one aspect of the problem. There is nothing to prevent these alternatives, such as romanticism as an alternative tendency within Enlightenment (Calhoun, 1995: 102), from becoming reified categories in and of themselves, reproducing the same predicament for critique. A temporalized model of structure and an appreciation of temporal complexity adds an important corrective to the argument.

Finally structure and agency, or structure and difference, can coexist only within a temporalized model of form. The space for alternatives is always presented in time; difference itself is temporal. It is dynamic rather than categorical; it occurs and recurs. Taken together, complexity, contingency and temporality reconstitute form in a manner consistent with difference. The possibility of critique from within is reclaimed, and with respect to music and art there are many opportunities for its exercise.

NOTES

1. A similar point is made by Andreas Huyssen (1986) in his consideration of the postmodern. His thesis is that aesthetic postmodernism

has been a recuperative project, a search for tradition as much as a projection into the future, which also involves a rethinking of the nature of progress. This, in his view, defines an important distinction between modernity and postmodernity. I would alter this conception slightly to suggest that the type of temporal complexity Huyssen associates with postmodernism is always present, regardless of whether or not it is entertained in academic or aesthetic discourse or in the discourse of social institutions.

2. Even less systematic models of complexity have presented problems for the structure of critique. See, for instance, Nancy Fraser's (1989) criticism of the lack of normative grounds for critique in Foucault's work.

3. A structural similarity obtains between dialectics and contingency as forms of distinction. Both Adorno's articulation of identity and nonidentity and Luhmann's self-reference versus external reference are versions of simultaneous reference to self and to something else and demonstrate the two-sided character of distinction. However, the way these distinctions are operationalized is radically different, given the contexts in which they occur. In the context of a totalizing social system, autonomy is the condition in which art follows its own internal logic rather than the logic of commodity capitalism, the logic of domination. It is art that is not colonized by the culture industry, nor does it reproduce bourgeois ideology or the ideology of the workplace. However it may have been articulated as an abstract form, within the context of the totally administered world, autonomy as identity is largely nonidentity—a self as distinct from an overarching or totalizing social system. The dynamic or contested aspect of the dialectic, the tension between identity and nonidentity, could not be sustained in this context. On the other hand, in systems theory, identity is not self-reference as opposed to external reference but the difference between self-reference and external reference as it is continually reproduced in communications within the subsystem. Identity is framed as the distinction itself. Similarly, closure (the system's difference from its environment) is not an end in itself but the condition of possibility for openness. This is what Luhmann calls "accompanying," as distinct from totalizing, self-reference ([1984] 1995: 447). The difference between these two conceptualizations is clear with respect to the autonomy status of art. In Luhmann's analysis, the development of self-referential subsystems has opened up the possibilities of system actualizations (self-reference and social function are mutually implied), whereas in the dialectical model those possibilities compromise autonomy (which is equated with the absence of social function).

4. This was quite a departure from the earlier vision of domination in modern society, illustrated in his analysis of 12-tone composition, in which there are no relations between tones; tones are related only to the row that dominates them. For more detailed analysis, see Hanrahan (1989).

5. Nevertheless, in lieu of creating new possibilities for critique through a different conception of context, this position signaled a retreat from the possibility of synthesis. Unity or totality had totalitarian implications. At the same time, however, that Adorno took the side of the nonidentical, he retained the idea of reconciliation and redemptive criticism.

6. In many respects, Luhmann's account of differentiation in the modern period is a dialog with Weber. Here the thesis of rationalization of value spheres is particularly pertinent; see *Rational and Social Foundations of Music* (1958).

7. The explanation that follows does not engage other sociological models of time and temporal complexity, including those of Norbert Elias (1992), who was both concerned with taking apart the dichotomies of nature versus culture with respect to time and in developing a process sociology; Barbara Adam (1995), who considered the multiplicity and mutual implication of natural, cultural and social times; and Reinhart Koselleck (1985), whose work explores ideas such as the contemporaneity of the noncontemporaneous and the space of experience within the horizon of expectation. All of these authors frame temporal complexity as either multiple forms of time within the present or layered forms of time reckoning. They are certainly important arguments but not specifically useful to the question of the temporal structure of critique.

8. This tension may be a result of the combination of theoretical models that Luhmann uses: both phenomenology, though he is careful to distance himself from what he calls transcendental phenomenology, and an information-processing model, from which he later distanced himself, considering it too simplistic.

9. This problem has been reproduced in, among others, the debates over a feminist standpoint. Is there such a thing as "women's knowledge"? Can it be articulated in terms other than those of the available knowledge base? If not, if women's knowledge is an alternative latent in the system, does that compromise its critical function? Wolff (1990) presents an overview of these arguments.

10. Although, as Fraser (1989) notes, the transition is not at all clear in Foucault's analysis.

11. This is true not only of the structures generated by social systems but also of systems of language and music, in which structures of meaning are constitutive aspects of communication but do not produce given communications.

5

BEYOND DIALECTICS

Temporality, complexity and contingency speak not only to the question of critique from within but also to the postmodern criticism that critique is ideological and unable to account for difference. Temporal models of form produce categories that are themselves dynamic and cannot be articulated solely through formal aesthetic properties. Temporality in music, for instance, is both formal and experiential, historical and phenomenological. These temporal distinctions cut across the hierarchical divide of art versus entertainment, of classical versus popular music. To the extent that all music articulates time, all music is process, temporal categories allow us to consider all forms of music without subjecting them to the formal imperatives of any specific one. In other words, temporal categories circumvent the problematic of universalism and relativism.

TIME AND CONTENT

In the sociological analysis of music, Weber's *The Rational and Social Foundations of Music* (1958) and Adorno's *Philosophy of Modern Music* ([1948] 1973) provide an illuminating contrast between the use of spatial and temporal models. Weber constructed a homology between the system of chordal harmony in Western music and rationalized forms of social organization. In order to make the argument, he used conventional forms of musicological analysis, which emphasize the relations between notes in a tonal system and their vertical arrangement. The analysis is hierarchical in a double sense: because chordal structure was its subject and because no other musical system, to Weber's knowledge, demonstrated these same highly rationalized characteristics. For Adorno, on the other hand, compositional process is the source of musical meaning. He analyzed Arnold Schoenberg's compositional forms (atonal and 12-tone), which eschewed the system of chordal harmony. In the atonal work, tonal relations are not vertical but horizontal, which allows for free expression. However, Adorno criticized Schoenberg's later 12-tone composition precisely as a reification of formal technique in which meaningful process was no longer possible. Twelve-tone music, as an analog to social organization, is authoritarian in that there are no relations between tones; all tones relate only to the row that dominates them. In this highly spatial model of composition, music becomes static and, according to Adorno, denies history.[1]

In Adorno's many analyses of music, autonomy became the content of critique. Autonomy was the criterion of good music in that it kept open the possibility of nonidentity with respect to social steering mechanisms, and of autonomous thought and subjectivity. In my conceptualization, time becomes content, and temporal complexity the criterion of good music in that it opens up the space for alternatives. Sustained temporal complexity also generates the space for reflection, which was the mediating category of critique (between subject and object) in the dialectical model. Thus reflection is not dependent on specific aesthetic forms or forms of logic; rather, it is a noninstrumental relation to time and is dependent on surprise.

According to many musicians, what makes music musical is its relation to time. When musicians in jazz, for instance, say that someone was playing a lot of "music," they don't mean that the person played a lot of notes. As Miles Davis in his better moments made clear, it is possible to play very little and yet to play plenty of music. Like the best jazz singers, Miles' phrasing worked against the meter and across the bar lines. He also frequently played with a mute, which diffused the sound of the trumpet rather than stating it in a sharp, clean attack. On Teo Macero's "Jack Johnson" (1970), for instance, these elements are juxtaposed against an accompaniment of sustained chords. Repetition serves in this instance as extension, as continual projection rather than a return to an original point. The piece is the result of a process in which Macero wrote for Miles' sound and then used a variety of production and editing techniques to get the intended results. The sparse openness is part of Miles' musical signature.

What made Miles' playing so musical was the way it articulated time. Yet time and space are mutually implied. Musicality opens out time, but in so doing it also situates the listener. Music that is musical arrests our attention, holds us on its terrain. However it is accomplished stylistically, reinvented time also creates a unique and eventful sense of place. On the other hand, if music is not musical, its moments become reified as an expression of situation alone.

Music that is rhythmically simple and repetitive, as is a great deal of commercial music of all sorts, is not bad music because it is entertainment, because it is a commodity, because it is a reproduction of the workplace to fill leisure time or because it turns listeners into mindless idiots. However, it is often distinctly unmusical because it admits of no other possibility than indication in the present. Take for example, Madonna's "Skin" on *Ray of Light* (1998). Even though the music is driven by an incessant up-tempo dance beat, it is remarkably static. Drum machines generate a rhythm that doesn't breathe, that reproduces time rather than articulating it. Repetition, therefore, is not projection but simply restates situation. Madonna's voice is recorded with a lot of echo, trying for the same diffused effect on the voice as the mute has on the trumpet. That is also the intention behind devices like a stop and restart in the middle of the song, and fading the voice and other synthesized effects in and out over the rhythm. These register as effects rather than as an integral part of the music in that they do nothing to alter the statement of time. In lieu of articulating or inventing time, the piece merely restates the present through an unchanging rhythmic pattern and an aggregate of different effects.

The question for critique is, simply, what is it? It is certainly a translation of money into music. There are no mistakes or rough spots, and it was produced with top-of-the-line technology. There is also no doubt that the recording took a great deal of time, not only because that would be the norm for someone with as much industry clout as Madonna but also because the techniques involved in producing this kind of sound are sophisticated. One can only imagine how many lawyers were involved in the contract negotiations, how many record company executives argued with her over what they thought they could sell. All of these translations may be successful to one degree or another. However, music that is unmusical, that does not reinvent time, is quickly drained of its eventfulness and most nearly attains the status of a bounded or stable object.

If, on the other hand, musicality is established, critique turns to the question of complexity, to exactly how the complexity of time is generated or sustained. Temporal complexity is situated through its eventfulness, through opening out the present to that which is not present, and sustained complexity is dependent upon surprise. It is surprise that problematizes all other temporal references. Surprise drives a wedge through the present, producing astonishment or simply the need to normalize radically new information. Temporally understood, it creates radical discontinuity. However, music need not be technically or formally (i.e., compositionally) sophisticated in order to be temporally complex. Time is articulated not only through rhythm and phrasing but also experientially in the listening process.

Temporal complexity is both experiential and formal in Kip Hanrahan's ". . . she turned so that maybe a third of her face was in this fuckin' beautiful half-light . . ." on *Tenderness* (1990a). The trap drummer on this guaguanco is playing three rhythms including the clave, the quinto (the top hand drum) solos, while one of the basses plays the overtones of the middle hand drum. Two additional basses play straight fours on top of the guaguanco ensemble. What makes the piece surprising is that expectations of where the melody and the rhythm are played are inverted; even the violin is playing a drum rhythm. It is also surprising in that the multiple rhythms are displaced from the conventional guaguanco setting, with each instrument assigned a part that it would not normally play. In this case, the added rhythms in straight four do not define the piece, reducing all of the rhythmic complexity to a pop format. In fact, it is almost impossible to count the fours in the density of the rhythm. The relation between the two musical styles is structural—they are both changed in the process. This piece segues into ". . . at the same time, as the subway train was pulling out of the station . . ." (1990b) a tanga which similarly reconfigures the traditional rhythms and adds free jazz piano on top. There are vocals on both pieces, in the first instance half-sung, half-spoken; in the second, whispered over against the rhythm. The words themselves are self-contradictory and describe an internal dissonance. There is a repetition of form in both pieces, but the music remains continuously eventful. Within that form, with every repetition, there are always new things being played, and the complexity of the rhythmic juxtaposition is always surprising. At any of its moments, time is multiply articulated and with all those drums, it's like a tangible, sensual force. It is music that is both knowledgeable about and critical of the conventions (Latin, jazz and rock) it employs; a music that continually creates alternatives.

Nothing is more surprising than rhythmic complexity, in that all of the aspects of musical time—the historical, the compositional, the experiential and the processual—are brought into play. Conversely, nothing is as bound to the idea of stasis or repetition as rhythm. A shift in musical analysis from harmonic complexity to rhythmic complexity is imperative for critique if it is to open up the junctures and discontinuities of musical time. Western classical music has been formalized as harmonically complex yet rhythmically rather predictable. Rock or popular musics may present many innovations, but they hardly challenge that premise. The argument being made here is not that non-Western musics in toto are rhythmically more complex—indeed, many are constructed through the decidedly simple repetition of rhythmic patterns. Rather, music that is temporally complex problematizes rhythm, makes of it more than the patterned marking of musical time, or a groove, or a set of static references that frame melodic or harmonic activity. Musical time is more than the parameter within which music takes place.

As a general trend, the world beat experiment in popular music has played around the edges of this problem. The idea of borrowing from other musical traditions, particularly the "folk" or "ethnic" musics of the non-West, opens up the possibility of introducing a measure of rhythmic complexity into what is a highly patterned popular form. Yet in lieu of achieving genuine complexity, what normally has resulted is a form of exotica. Paul Simon's *Graceland* (1986) is a case in point. For the most part, the songs on this record are Simon's (indeed, he owns all the publishing) and do not vary in style or form from what he would have written without the participation of Ladysmith Black Mambazo, the South African vocal group that appears on the recording. In lieu of using the South African style of rhythmic singing to reinvent compositional form, it appears as something extra—a frill or an exotic touch. In this sense it is representative of the great failure of this work; that is, its inability to problematize either the Western popular music or the "exotic" rhythms it imports. Adding a conga player to a drum machine track leaves all of our presuppositions, cultural and temporal, intact. The vocal cadence of Ofra Haza, a Yemenite Israeli singer, superimposed over a rock beat allows us to have a cross-cultural experience without ever leaving the comfort of our expectations or our living rooms (*Fifty Gates of Wisdom*, 1987). Whatever the intent, be it, as in Haza's case, an interest in blending the traditional songs of her Yemenite Jewish heritage with a more popular beat, or simply the conforming of all musical traditions to the financial imperatives of the pop market, the results have been stunningly similar. As exotica rather than reinvention, there is no temporal complexity, and what at first seem to be surprising juxtapositions are quickly normalized in the absence of a more structural disjunction. In other words, there are no real alternatives.

Finally, it demonstrates how difficult it is to project a future that does not yet exist, to open out the possibilities of time and the alternatives latent within it. Adorno was in fact deeply concerned with a different aspect of this problem. He criticized Schoenberg's 12-tone composition for what he understood to be a reification of technique to the point of formal, compositional stasis. What Schoenberg ([1975] 1984) described as the unity of musical space, in which there is no absolute up or down, forward or backward, and in which every musical configuration resonates in multiple times and places, Adorno dismissed as only geometrical symmetry. To a large extent, Adorno was right. Many of the strictly composed 12-tone pieces are "constructed to death" (Adorno, [1948] 1973: 100) and neither processual nor expressive. Yet the end of compositional process is not history coming to a standstill. Rather, it is music that has only a present. It has lost its temporality and therefore cannot present a space for alternatives or function as critique.

None of the temporal categories used in this analysis function as high art categories that are necessarily compromised by the presence of translations from the environment, such as money and technology. In fact, all of these examples were recorded, so both money and technology were involved. They become more important to critique in the instances where musicality and temporal complexity are lacking. In addition, these temporal categories can be applied to every kind, sort, genre or style of music, to the extent that all music is process and is realized in time. The categories presented here do not reproduce the "high art" versus entertainment paradigm, nor are they situated on the aesthetic terrain of Western classical music. Granted, a criterion of good music as unpredictable, processual and temporally complex functions in this critique, but it does not constitute a new hierarchy because these categories are contingent and context dependent. For instance, pop music, which is often severely constrained by form, can be very musical (great singers like Willie Nelson come to mind), or complex, like Ani DiFranco. Her "Shy" (on *Not a Pretty Girl*, 1995) provides an interesting example. Formally, it is a rather conventional pop song—a repeated rhythm in four. However, the accented notes on the guitar don't lock with the expectations of the form. In addition, DiFranco sings from her throat, and because the voice is recorded flat, with no echo, her breathing is audible. So whether she whispers or shouts, it takes the vocal lines off the beat. The net effect is that time is stretched in unpredictable ways, as guitar and voice often pull against each other.

Temporal categories are fluid and open-ended; because time in music is more than purely formal, it cannot be stabilized in compositional form. Unlinked from the predispositions of genre, the categories of critique become more contingent upon what one hears. There is no retreat; critique involves both commitment and risk.

FORM AND CONCEPT

I have argued that the utility of a critical project in aesthetics is the consideration of form and that a critical project in music illuminates its temporality. The formal contributions of my work to critical theory and cultural sociology can be summarized as follows. First, dialectics is an inadequate conception of social or cultural processes. Instead, processes are contingent in that they are nonlinear, paradoxical and open to anomalous occurrences; they could always have turned out otherwise. Second, temporalized language and analytical categories are necessary to deal with the complexity of social and cultural phenomena, just as temporalized forms are necessary to preserve both structure and difference within a single model. As a corollary, the notion of difference as difference in and of itself, or as cultural specificity, is replaced with the concept of contingent differentiation. Finally, my work has examined the temporal structure of critique and demonstrated that contingency and difference, far from being antithetical to critique, are in fact its preconditions.

In the Introduction, I suggested that scholars in critical theory have made substantial breakthroughs in integrating certain questions, particularly of feminism, within its framework. In a manner consistent with the tradition of critical theory itself, feminist scholars have critiqued and reinterpreted existing analytical categories (Nicholson, 1987; Fraser, 1987) and added or adapted new forms of analysis, such as discourse theory (Fraser, 1989) and poststructuralism (Scott, 1994), to critique. They have also remained true to the interdisciplinary project of critical theory, using the best available materials in the social sciences and humanities to further research. Yet the aesthetic project, with its considerations of both form and time, has a great deal to contribute to questions that have emerged in both feminist critical theory and in sociological analysis more generally, concerning the relation between culture and political economy, between solidarity and difference and between cultural difference and aesthetic critique. The following brief sketch will draw out some of the implications of my work and suggest ways in which it can be applied to analytical problems in cultural sociology and feminist theory.

DIALECTICS

Liberal feminism as it developed in the 1960s was organized around the goals of equality of economic opportunity and equal participation in public life. To the extent that exclusion and inequality are supported by assumptions about what women are like, how they are expected to behave, or social ideals of femininity, the struggle for equality takes place not only in the political arena but also in the cultural one. In the construction of new social roles for women, collective forms of representation are iconic. In recent years, depictions of the working mother, the female cop, the corporate executive whose husband stays home with the baby, the opinionated working-class woman, the liberated call girl and the feminist politician have all appeared on television and in film. What is the relationship between cultural representations and real social struggles? Where are these depictions coming from, and by what type of process are they produced? Is there some kind of dialectic at work between emergent social roles and the representation of those roles? Certainly, Hollywood is reacting to ongoing cultural creativity and social change, but it also participates in it. The more those roles are depicted, however mediated by the culture industry, the more available they become as a ground of contestation. They would not have much currency, however, nor would they be profitable, if they were not tapping into an existent social struggle. The process is multidirectional. The modernist narrative of cultural manipulation would suggest that the culture industry is exploiting these new social roles for profit at the same time that it privatizes the underlying social issues and conflicts, presenting them in the context of individual life stories. The alternative narrative of reception as social agency might suggest that Hollywood is responding to changes in its audience as well as audience demands for legitimate representation. Neither, however, adequately explains this phenomenon.

Yet posing the relationship between political economy and culture in this instance as a dialectic between these two narratives is also inadequate. In the absence of the teleology of synthesis or resolution, dialectics has come to mean simply that both aspects have to be taken into account, without clarifying the form of their relation. In this case, there are also multiple (as opposed to two) variables in play that neither narrative incorporates. For example, the social struggle itself is polyvalent. It includes not only feminist practice vis-à-vis existing cultural representations but also struggles among feminists to define these roles and the social changes they require, as well as between feminists and nonfeminists who perceive new social roles as a threat to traditional notions of domesticity. At the same time, the culture industry is not, as I have argued, streamlined in either its decision making or its production methods. It is always playing with (or against) risk, and its products are the result of highly contingent and often irrational processes. Finally, the outcomes for women are far more complex than a dialectical model would suggest. Rather than a clear trajectory of progress, as cultural representations and social roles proliferate, women may have more options, but they also face more role conflict and a stronger backlash. In fact, it is less and less clear, in the landscape of cultural representation, what constitutes liberation and what reproduces repression. Cultural creativity yields greater complexity but not necessarily liberation.

DIFFERENCE, COMPLEXITY AND TIME

Social movements often reproduce the very conflicts they seek to redress because they are generated within and cannot escape elements of the larger culture. Feminism is no exception, having faced the dilemma of inclusion and exclusion as an aspect of both institutional and symbolic representation. After the first phase of feminism, led by a predominantly white, middle-class and educated group of women, many lesbians, working-class women and women of color claimed that the movement represented neither their interests nor their experience. Feminism had been so concerned with the question of women's oppression and women's inequality vis-à-vis a patriarchal system of domination that it had failed to recognize differences between women themselves. The category *women* as an all-inclusive one certainly had strategic value in galvanizing the movement in its early stages of formation, but at a later stage it either had to be abandoned by feminists or become a subject for reflection about feminism's racial, class, sexual and ideological construction.

As the discussion of gender difference shifted to the terrain of differences among women, the category *women* also shifted. It became gay or straight; professional, working or domestic; black or Asian or Latina or white; working class or upper class; first world or third world; pro-choice or pro-life; and so on. One possible interpretation is that the category fell apart, and with it any notion of solidarity. Suffice it to say that the situation has been widely perceived as a problem of balkanization. Yet none of these categories of *woman* are mutually exclusive, nor do they deny a broader solidarity. An alternative explanation of the relationship between difference and solidarity is possible if the problem is given a temporal interpretation.

Both observation and experience demonstrate that differences among women are not just differences per se, but differences which generate more differences. Dynamic cultural processes tend to produce difference in the continual refinement and critique of existing social and cultural categories. Further, there is no part-to-whole relation in which differences like black and white women, or working-class or professional women, constitute smaller components or subsets of a larger category of women. This is so because these differences are related not only to the larger category but also to each other. There are in fact multiple possible relations between the parts and therefore no fixed boundaries between categories of difference. That is the definition of complexity.

Women, then, is a complex form of difference that will continue to generate difference. Further, given a temporalized model of form rather than a static one, it no longer makes sense to conceptualize difference as a negative principle to the positive one of solidarity (which is, in fact, very dialectical in construction). In a part-to-whole model, solidarity is the condition in which the parts add up to a whole. In a temporalized model, the whole is constantly emerging through the dynamic relations of the parts. Like difference, solidarity is subject to ongoing articulation and construction. Solidarity is not the opposite of difference but an emergent form of complexity, which in turn is possible only because difference exists.[2]

What have been the consequences of this growing complexity for feminism? Nancy Fraser suggests that by around 1990 "the decisive U.S. feminist debate was poised to shift from 'differences among women' to 'multiple intersecting differences'" (1997: 180), which could have been a tremendous gain. The discussion could be resituated in a political field that was now more complex, "where multiple axes of difference were being contested simultaneously and where multiple social movements were intersecting" (180). What organizes this conceptualization is the notion of "interimbrication," or the interweaving of cultural and social demands. Given a complex political field, in which there are multiple axes of domination, demands for social equality cut across demands for cultural recognition. Yet what has occurred instead, according to Fraser, has been an almost exclusive turn among feminists to the cultural side, resulting in a fruitless debate between multiculturalism and antiessentialism. Why would this be the case?

If complexity is viewed as a process rather than as a condition or, in this case, as the intersection of multiple differences, the explanation is readily available. Increasing complexity enforces selection, without which the amount of information or the number of variables cannot be managed. The inward turn among feminists to questions of cultural recognition and identity is an example of this phenomenon. As the political field became more complex, feminists selected out those issues and problems most central to the internal constitution of feminism. This reduced the number of variables vis-à-vis the broader political field but simultaneously created the conditions in which these central issues could be considered in ever more complex forms. The terrain shifted from a discussion of gender difference or differences among women to the structure and politics of difference itself.[3]

As an aside, temporalized language also has implications for the language of everyday politics. Political orientations that formerly were identified through temporal designations such as *progressive* and *conservative* have been replaced by spatial terms— *left* and *right*. As political positions become more complex, left and right become increasingly meaningless in the description of social movements, some of which, like the ecology movement, are both progressive and conservative. In her work on redistribution and recognition, Fraser (1997) introduces the temporally descriptive terminology of transformative and affirmative tendencies, which could have broad utility.

CULTURAL DIFFERENCE / AESTHETIC CRITIQUE

My contribution to the critical theory project has been to suggest alternative models of form and to reveal the possibilities of a more temporalized language both for the sake of accuracy and as a way of coping with dualisms such as universalism and relativism or structure and difference. These theoretical alterations also address the specific argument that aesthetic critique is based on universal categories and cannot accomodate cultural difference, which is presented as a form of relativism. Contrary to this argument, difference is compatible with the temporal structure of critique in that difference is continually and contingently produced, and is a precondition of critique in that alternatives are always differences in time. As a corollary, both rigid aesthetic categories and a priori cultural distinctions are antithetical to critique in that they are static articulations of difference. The unresolved dualism of critique, that of aesthetic judgment based on universal categories and standpoint relative to specific cultural, ethnic, gender or identity groups, turns out to be false when critique is understood as a dynamic and contingent process in which both judgment and standpoint are emergent.

CONCLUSION

In "Meaning as Sociology's Basic Concept," Luhmann wrote:

The term *complexity* is meant to indicate that there are always more possibilities of experience and action than can be actualized. The term *contingency* is intended to express the fact that the possibilities of further experience and action indicated in the horizon of actual experience are just that—possibilities—and might turn out differently than expected, i.e., that these indications can be deceptive: perhaps they point to something that is not really there or cannot be reached in the way expected; perhaps even after the necessary steps have been taken (e.g., someone has gone to a particular place) what was expected can no longer be actualized, because events in the meantime have removed or destroyed this possibility. In practice then, complexity means the necessity of choosing; contingency, the necessity of accepting risks. (1990: 26)

Critique necessitates both choice and risk. It is a process of making distinctions and judgments, of making choices. In Hannah Arendt's model of politics, and in the model of critique as it has been envisioned here, these choices are not made from a safe distance but in the presence of others. The risks include that of convincing or failing to convince others, of being proven right or wrong and of distinguishing oneself while still taking others into account. They also include the risk of uncertainty, of unknowable outcomes.

Complexity and contingency describe social structure and social process. Critique has to be formulated within this model if we are to do justice both to new conceptions of social reality and to ongoing social practice. Temporality is central to understanding how the space for alternatives continues to arise, even in unfavorable circumstances. Viewed against this, dialectics appears functionalist in that it is premised on binary rather than complex relations; although it recognizes temporal distinctions between what is and what ought to be, it is teleological rather than contingent. It makes choices but doesn't accept risk. On the other hand, postmodern theory grasps complexity but without the understanding that it necessitates choice; it recognizes contingency, but contingency is meaningless if no choices are being made.

Postmodernists have argued that the contingency and complexity of social organization and analytical categories signal the death of critique on the grounds that neither orthodox political commitments nor universal aesthetic categories any longer provide recourse to the truth. Cultural conservatives have said that without appeal to those standards, judgment is not possible, and the consequences for both politics and culture are dire. Contrary to both sets of predictions, contingency, complexity, and temporality can generate a critique premised on difference that involves both commitment and risk.

NOTES

1. Reproducing either the structure of homology or the philosophy of history that guided Adorno's work would be very problematic. However, Adorno's intuition about musical structure and meaning as process has implications that he did not pursue in his analyses of other musical forms, like jazz, and which are interesting in this context.

2. The ramifications of this argument for work on identity construction should be evident. Identity is a process of generating complexity through ongoing differentiation, from which multiple forms of solidarity can then be produced.

3. It may well be that this inward turn is not irrevocable, but that the questions that are being engaged must either be resolved or exhausted before feminists as a whole turn their attention again to a larger conception of politics.

REFERENCES

Adam, Barbara. 1990. *Time and Social Theory*. Philadelphia: Temple University Press.

———. 1995. *Timewatch: The Social Analysis of Time*. Cambridge, UK: Polity Press.

Adorno, Theodor W. [1938] 1982. "On the Fetish Character in Music and the Regression of Listening," in Andrew Arato and Eike Gebhardt (eds.), *The Essential Frankfurt School Reader*. New York: Continuum.

———. [1948] 1973. *Philosophy of Modern Music*, trans. Anne G. Mitchell and Wesley V. Blomster. New York: Continuum.

———. [1962] 1976. *Introduction to the Sociology of Music*, trans. E. B. Ashton. New York: Seabury Press.

———. [1967] 1981. "Cultural Criticism and Society," in *Prisms*, trans. Samuel and Sherry Weber. Cambridge, MA: MIT Press.

———. [1970] 1984. *Aesthetic Theory*, trans. C. Lenhardt. London: Routledge and Kegan Paul.

———. [1973] 1983. *Negative Dialectics*, trans. E. B. Ashton. New York: Continuum.

Alexander, Christopher. 1964. *Notes on the Synthesis of Form*. Cambridge, MA: Harvard University Press.

Althusser, Louis. 1971. "Ideology and Ideological State Apparatuses," in *Lenin and Philosophy and Other Essays*, trans. Ben Brewster. London: New Left Books.

Arendt, Hannah. [1954] 1977a. "The Crisis in Culture," in *Between Past and Future*. New York: Penguin.

———. [1954] 1977b. "Truth and Politics," in *Between Past and Future*. New York: Penguin.

———. 1958. *The Human Condition*. Chicago: University of Chicago Press.

Bell, Daniel. 1976. *The Cultural Contradictions of Capitalism*. New York: Basic Books.

Bennett, Tony. 1995. *The Birth of the Museum*. London: Routledge.

Berezin, Mabel. 1997. *Making the Fascist Self: The Political Culture of Interwar Italy*. Ithaca: Cornell University Press.

Bergson, Henri. 1950. *Time and Free Will: An Essay on the Immediate Data of Consciousness*. New York: Humanities Press.

Bhabha, Homi. 1994. *The Location of Culture*. London: Routledge.

Blake, Casey Nelson. 1993. "An Atmosphere of Effrontery: Richard Serrs, Tilted Arc and the Crisis of Public Art," in Richard Wightman Fox and T. J. Jackson Lears (eds.), *The Power of Culture*. Chicago: University of Chicago Press.

Bloom, Allan. 1987. *The Closing of the American Mind: How Higher Education Has Failed Democracy and Impoverished the Souls of Today's Students*. New York: Simon and Schuster.

Bois, Yves-Alain. 1990. *Painting as Model*. Cambridge, MA: MIT Press.

Bourdieu, Pierre. 1984. *Distinction: A Social Critique of the Judgement of Taste*, trans. Richard Nice. Cambridge, MA: Harvard University Press.

———. 1993. "The Production of Belief: Contribution to the Economy of Symbolic Goods," in Randal Johnson (ed.), *The Field of Cultural Production: Essays on Art and Literature*. New York: Columbia University Press.

———. 1996. *The Rules of Art: Genesis and Structure of the Literary Field*, trans. Susan Emanuel. Stanford, CA: Stanford University Press.

Bourke, V. J. (ed.). 1983. *The Essential Augustine*. Indianapolis, IN: Hackett.

Bowler, Anne. 1992. "Art and Politics in the Historical Avant-Garde: Italian Futurism and Russian Constructivism." Ph.D. diss., New School for Social Research, New York.

Brown, G. Spencer. 1972. *Laws of Form*. New York: Julian Press.

Buck-Morss, Susan. 1977. *The Origin of the Negative Dialectic: Theodor W. Adorno, Walter Benjamin and the Frankfurt Institute*. New York: Free Press.

Burger, Peter. 1984. *Theory of the Avant-Garde*, trans. Michael Show. Minneapolis: University of Minnesota Press.

Burrows, David. 1990. *Sound, Speech and Music.* Amherst: University of Massachusetts Press.

Butler, Judith P. 1993. *Bodies That Matter: On the Discursive Limits of "Sex."* New York: Routledge.

Cage, John. 1973. *Silence.* Middletown, CT: Wesleyan University Press.

Calhoun, Craig. 1995. *Critical Social Theory.* Cambridge, MA: Blackwell.

Calinescu, Matei. 1987. "On Postmodernism," in *Five Faces of Modernity.* Durham, NC: Duke University Press.

Castoriadis, Cornelius. 1992. "The Retreat from Autonomy: Post-Modernism as Generalized Conformism." *Thesis Eleven* 31.

Cohen, Jean L., and Andrew Arato. 1992. *Civil Society and Political Theory.* Cambridge, MA: MIT Press.

Crane, Diana. 1992. *The Production of Culture: Media and the Urban Arts.* Newbury Park, CA: Sage.

DiMaggio, Paul. 1982. "Cultural Entrepreneurship in 19th Century Boston." *Media, Culture and Society* 4.

———. 1992. "Cultural Boundaries and Structural Change: The Extension of the High Culture Model to Theater, Opera, and Dance, 1900–1940," in Marcel Fournier and Michele Lamont (eds.), *Cultivating Differences: Symbolic Boundaries and the Making of Inequality.* Chicago: University of Chicago Press.

Dubin, Steve C. 1992. *Arresting Images: Impolitic Art and Uncivil Actions.* New York: Routledge.

Eagleton, Terry. 1990. *The Ideology of the Aesthetic.* Oxford, UK: Basil Blackwell.

Elias, Norbert. 1992. *Time: An Essay.* Oxford, UK: Basil Blackwell.

Feher, Ferenc. 1975. "Negative Philosophy of Music—Positive Results." *New German Critique* 4.

———. 1987. "Max Weber and the Rationalization of Music." *International Journal of Politics, Culture, and Society* 1 (2).

Fiedler, Leslie A. 1977. "Cross the Border—Close the Gap," in *A Fiedler Reader.* New York: Stein and Day.

Fiske, John. 1987. *Television Culture.* New York: Routledge.

———. 1992. "Cultural Studies and the Culture of Everyday Life," in Lawrence Grossberg et al. (eds.), *Cultural Studies.* New York: Routledge.

Foster, Hal (ed.). 1983. *The Anti-aesthetic: Essays on Postmodern Culture.* Port Townsend, WA: Bay Press.

Foucault, Michel. [1977] 1995. *Discipline and Punish: The Birth of the Prison,* trans. Alan Sheridan. New York: Vintage Books.

———. 1978. *History of Sexuality,* vol. 1, trans. Robert Hurley. New York: Random House.

Fraser, Nancy. 1987. "What's Critical about Critical Theory? The Case of Habermas and Gender," in Seyla Benhabib and Drucilla Cornell (eds.), *Feminism as Critique: On the Politics of Gender*. Minneapolis: University of Minnesota Press.

———. 1989. "Foucault on Modern Power: Empirical Insights and Normative Confusions," in *Unruly Practices: Power, Discourse, and Gender in Contemporary Social Theory*. Minneapolis: University of Minnesota Press.

———. 1997. *Justice Interruptus: Critical Reflections on the "Postsocialist" Condition*. London: Routledge.

Fraser, Nancy, and Linda Nicholson. 1994. "Social Criticism without Philosophy: An Encounter between Feminism and Postmodernism," in Steven Seidman (ed.), *The Postmodern Turn: New Perspectives on Social Theory*. Cambridge, UK: Cambridge Press.

Frith, Simon. 1996. *Performing Rites: On the Value of Popular Music*. Cambridge, MA: Harvard University Press.

Gans, Herbert J. 1974. *Popular Culture and High Culture: An Analysis and Evaluation of Taste*. New York: Basic Books.

Giddens, Anthony. 1984. *The Constitution of Society: Outline of the Theory of Structuration*. Berkeley: University of California Press.

Gitlin, Todd. 1985. *Inside Prime Time*. New York: Pantheon.

Goldfarb, Jeffrey C. 1982. *On Cultural Freedom: An Exploration of Public Life in Poland and America*. Chicago: University of Chicago Press.

———. 1991. *The Cynical Society: The Culture of Politics and the Politics of Culture in American Life*. Chicago: University of Chicago Press.

Habermas, Jürgen. 1981. "Modernity Versus Postmodernity." *New German Critique* 22.

———. 1984. *Theory of Communicative Action*, trans. Thomas McCarthy. Boston: Beacon Press.

Hall, Stuart. 1980. "Cultural Studies and the Center: Some Problematics and Problems," in Stuart Hall, Dorothy Hobson, Andrew Lowe, and Paul Willis (eds.), *Culture, Media, Language: Working Papers in Cultural Studies, 1972–1979*. London: Hutchinson.

Hanrahan, Nancy Weiss. 1989. "Negative Composition." *Philosophy and Social Criticism* 15 (3).

———. 1993. "Music Criticism?" Paper presented at American Sociological Association Annual Meeting, Miami.

Harding, Sandra. 1991. *Whose Science? Whose Knowledge?* Ithaca, NY: Cornell University Press.

Hassan, Ihab Habib. 1987. *The Postmodern Turn: Essays in Postmodern Theory and Culture*. Columbus: Ohio State University Press.

Heidegger, Martin. [1927] 1996. *Being and Time*, trans. Joan Stambaugh. Albany: State University of New York Press.

Hirsch, E. D. 1987. *Cultural Literacy: What Every American Needs to Know*. Boston: Houghton Mifflin.

Hooks, Bell. 1990. *Yearning: Race, Gender and Cultural Politics*. Boston: South End Press.

Horkheimer, Max. 1982. "Traditional and Critical Theory," in *Critical Theory*, trans. J O'Connell. New York: Continuum.

Horkheimer, Max, and Theodor W. Adorno. [1944] 1972. *Dialectic of Enlightenment*, trans. John Cumming. New York: Herder & Herder.

Hunter, Ian. 1992. "Aesthetics and Cultural Studies," in Lawrence Grossberg, Cary Nelson, and Paula A. Treichler (eds.), *The Cultural Studies Reader*. New York: Routledge.

Husserl, Edmund. [1964] 1991. *On the Phenomenology of the Consciousness of Internal Time*, trans. John Barnett Brough. Boston: Kluwer.

Huyssen, Andreas. 1986. *After the Great Divide: Modernism, Mass Culture, and Postmodernism*. Bloomington: Indiana University Press.

Koselleck, Reinhart. 1985. *Futures Past: On the Semantics of Historical Time*, trans. Keith Tribe. Cambridge, MA: MIT Press.

Lemert, Charles C. 1995. *Sociology after the Crisis*. Boulder, CO: Westview Press.

Leppert, Richard, and Susan McClary (eds.). 1987. *Music and Society: The Politics of Composition, Performance and Reception*. Cambridge, UK: Cambridge University Press.

Levine, Donald N. 1995. *Visions of the Sociological Tradition*. Chicago: University of Chicago Press.

Levine, Lawrence W. 1988. *Highbrow/Lowbrow: The Emergence of Cultural Hierarchy in America*. Cambridge, MA: Harvard University Press.

Luhmann, Niklas. 1982. *The Differentiation of Society*, trans. Stephen Holmes and Charles Larmore. New York: Columbia University Press.

———. [1984] 1995. *Social Systems*, trans. John Bednarz, Jr., and Dirk Baecker. Stanford, CA: Stanford University Press.

———. 1989. *Ecological Communication*, trans. John Bednarz, Jr. Chicago: University of Chicago Press.

———. 1990. *Essays on Self-Reference*. New York: Columbia University Press.

———. 1992. "The Concept of Society." *Thesis Eleven* 31.

Marcuse, Herbert. 1964. *One-Dimensional Man: Studies in the Ideology of Advanced Industrial Society*. Boston: Beacon Press.

———. [1968] 1988. "The Struggle Against Liberalism in the Totalitarian View of the State," in *Negations: Essays in Critical Theory*, trans. Jeremy J. Shapiro. Boston: Beacon Press.

Marx, Karl. [1843] 1975a. "Letters from the Franco-German Yearbooks," in *Karl Marx: Early Writings*. New York: Vintage Books.

———. [1843] 1975b. "On the Jewish Question," in *Karl Marx: Early Writings*. New York: Vintage Books.

———. [1844] 1975. "Economic and Philosophical Manuscripts," in *Karl Marx: Early Writings*. New York: Vintage Books.

Mead, George Herbert. [1932] 1959. *The Philosophy of the Present*. La Salle, IL: Open Court.

Meyer, Leonard B. 1956. *Emotion and Meaning in Music*. Chicago: University of Chicago Press.

Nicholson, Linda. 1987. "Feminism and Marx: Integrating Kinship with the Economic," in Seyla Benhabib and Drucilla Cornell (eds.), *Feminism as Critique: On the Politics of Gender*. Minneapolis: University of Minnesota Press.

Ortega y Gasset, Jose. 1932. *The Revolt of the Masses*. New York: W. W. Norton.

Penley, Constance. 1992. "Feminism, Psychoanalysis, and the Study of Popular Culture," in Lawrence Grossberg et al. (eds.), *Cultural Studies*. New York: Routledge.

Peterson, Richard A. 1978. "The Production of Cultural Change: The Case of Contemporary Country Music." *Social Research* 45 (2).

Peterson, Richard (ed.). 1976. *The Production of Culture*. Beverly Hills, CA: Sage.

Prigogine, Ilya, and Isabelle Stengers. 1984. *Order out of Chaos: Man's New Dialogue with Nature*. New York: Bantam Books.

Radway, Janice A. 1984. *Reading the Romance: Women, Patriarchy, and Popular Literature*. Chapel Hill: University of North Carolina Press.

Ricoeur, Paul. [1983] 1984. *Time and Narrative*, trans. Kathleen McLaughlin and David Pellauer. Chicago: University of Chicago Press.

Schoenberg, Arnold. [1975] 1984. "Composition with 12 Tones (1)," in Leonard Stein (ed.), *Style and Idea: Selected Writings of Arnold Schoenberg*, trans. Leo Black. Berkeley: University of California Press.

Scott, Joan Wallach. 1989. *Gender and the Politics of History*. New York: Columbia University Press.

———. 1994. "Deconstructing Equality Versus Difference: On the Uses of Poststructuralist Theory for Feminism," in Steven Seidman (ed.), *The Postmodern Turn: New Perspectives on Social Theory*. Cambridge, UK: Cambridge Press.

Seidman, Steven. 1997. "Relativizing Sociology: The Challenge of Cultural Studies," in Elizabeth Long (ed.), *From Sociology to Cultural Studies*. Cambridge, MA: Blackwell.

Smith, Dorothy. 1987. *The Everyday World as Problematic: A Feminist Sociology*. Boston: Northeastern University Press.

Sontag, Susan. 1966. *Against Interpretation*. New York: Farrar Straus Giroux.

Spivak, Gayatri. 1988. "Can the Subaltern Speak?" in C. Nelson and L. Grossberg (eds.), *Marxism and the Interpretation of Culture*. Urbana: University of Illinois Press.

Subotnik, Rose Rosengard. 1991. *Developing Variations: Style and Ideology in Western Music*. Minneapolis: University of Minnesota Press.

Swiss, Thomas, John Sloop, and Andrew Herman (eds.). 1998. *Mapping the Beat: Popular Music and Contemporary Theory*. Malden, MA: Blackwell.

Weber, Max. 1930. *The Protestant Ethic and the Spirit of Capitalism*, trans. Talcott Parsons. London: Routledge.

———. 1958. *The Rational and Social Foundations of Music*, trans. Don Martindale, Johannes Riedel, and Gertrude Neuwirth (eds.). Carbondale: Southern Illinois University Press.

Wellmer, Albrecht. [1969] 1971. *Critical Theory of Society*, trans. John Cumming. New York: Seabury Press.

———. 1984. "Truth, Semblance and Reconciliation," in *Telos* 62.

Williams, Raymond. 1958. *Culture and Society, 1780–1950*. New York: Columbia University Press.

———. 1961. *The Long Revolution*. London: Penguin.

Williams-Crenshaw, Kimberle. 1997. "Beyond Racism and Misogyny: Black Feminism and 2 Live Crew," in *Feminist Social Thought: A Reader*. New York: Routledge.

Willis, Paul. 1977. *Learning to Labor: How Working Class Kids Get Working Class Jobs*. New York: Columbia University Press.

Wolff, Janet. 1981. *The Social Production of Art*. New York: St. Martin's Press.

———. 1990. *Feminine Sentences: Essays on Women and Culture*. Berkeley: University of California Press.

———. 1992. "Excess and Inhibition: Interdisciplinarity and the Study of Art," in Lawrence Grossberg, Cary Nelson, and Paula A. Treichler (eds.), *The Cultural Studies Reader*. New York: Routledge.

———. 1993. *Aesthetics and the Sociology of Art*, 2nd ed. Ann Arbor: University of Michigan Press.

Zerubavel, Eviatar. 1985. *The Seven Day Circle: The History and Meaning of the Week*. New York: Free Press.

———. 1991. *The Fine Line: Making Distinctions in Everyday Life*. New York: Free Press.

Zolberg, Vera L. 1990. *Constructing a Sociology of the Arts*. Cambridge, UK: Cambridge University Press.

———. 1992. "Barrier or Leveler? The Case of the Art Museum," in Marcel Fournier and Michele Lamont (eds.), *Cultivating Differences: Symbolic Boundaries and the Making of Inequality*. Chicago: University of Chicago Press.

DISCOGRAPHY

DiFranco, Ani. 1995. "Shy," on *Not a Pretty Girl*. Buffalo, NY: Righteous Babe Music.

Hanrahan, Kip. 1990a. ". . . she turned so that maybe a third of her face was in this fuckin' beautiful half-light . . ." on *Tenderness*. Reston, VA: American Clave.

———. 1990b. ". . . at the same time, as the subway train was pulling out of the station . . . ," on *Tenderness*. Reston, VA: American Clave.

Haza, Ofra. 1987. *Fifty Gates of Wisdom*. New York: Shanachie Records.

Macero, Teo. 1970. "Jack Johnson." Unreleased recording. New York.

Madonna. 1998. "Skin," on *Ray of Light*. New York: Maverick, WB Records.

Simon, Paul. 1986. *Graceland*. New York: Warner Brothers.

INDEX

About the Author

NANCY WEISS HANRAHAN is Associate Professor of Sociology at George Mason University. Before entering academia, she worked in the music business as a radio announcer and as a program director of New Jazz at the Public, a concert series of jazz and experimental music in New York City.

ISBN 0-275-96975-4

90000>

EAN

9 780275 969752

HARDCOVER BAR CODE